Acrobat Music

By the same author:

The Mask and the Jagged Star
Flagging Down Time
The Book of Possibilities
Screens Jets Heaven: New and Selected Poems
Broken/Open
Dark Bright Doors
Ash is Here, So are Stars
The Beautiful Anxiety
Breaking the Days
Brink
Viva the Real
A History Of What I'll Become
Wild Curious Air

I acknowledge that this book was assembled on the unceded lands of the Kaurna people, and I pay my respects to their elders, past and present.

Acrobat Music
New & Selected Poems

Jill Jones

PUNCHER & WATTMANN

First published in 2023 by Puncher and Wattmann
PO Box 279
Waratah NSW 2298

http://www.puncherandwattmann.com

info@puncherandwattmann.com

NATIONAL
LIBRARY
OF AUSTRALIA

A catalogue entry for this book is available from the National Library of

Australia.

ISBN 9781922571571

Cover design by David Musgrave
Cover image: Fearful Symmetry, Berlin, 2016 ©Annette Willis, 2016.

Reproduced with permission.

Printed by Lightning Source International

This project has been assisted by the Australian Government through the Australia Council, its arts funding and advisory body.

Australian Government

Australia Council
for the Arts

Contents

2. *It is impossible to live as if we are free*

3. clear, grey light falls forever …

4. the way the air touches you …

The new poems

Author's Foreword

I have published 13 full-length books between 1992 and 2020, as well as any number of poems from the mid-1980s. The number 13 is personally significant to me, so that fact, plus the inevitable passing of time, encouraged me to put together this volume. Some of my books are still in print, and of course all the books preferably should be experienced in full. However, not everyone would wish to nor be able to track them all down. Just under half of them are now out of print and most are not readily available second-hand.

Each of my books had its own approach, although none of them has been, in the narrow sense, a 'project'. The thinking that drew each book together related either to an interest in certain formal or thematic preoccupations, a summing up of a period of writing, or sometimes just a feeling towards a particular stance to language and/or theme. The closest of my books to follow any kind of project idea is *Breaking the Days*, consisting of poems of one page or less (plus a long sequence of very short poems), and where some of the shorter poems were first posted on social media. To a lesser extent, *A History Of What I'll Become*, *Wild Curious Air*, and *Ash is Here, So are Stars*, all have certain concepts of order.

Extracting poems from their arrangement within a single book to make this kind of volume is a disruption. I could have adopted the time-honoured chronological method, by including poems from each book from the oldest to most recent. However, as there would already be a disruption via such a selection, plus the fact that a chronology doesn't fit how I see my work, I have clustered the collected poems across five very broad areas or zones, with the sixth part consisting of new, ie uncollected or unpublished, poems. Despite variations in my personal style and interests, as well as changes in age and circumstance, I wanted to show, through this form of clustering, what I have been doing for the three or so decades I've been publishing. In effect, I wanted to make this a new book in and of itself. Of course, a number of poems could have been placed in more than one of these areas/zones; my choice was sometimes based simply on the soundings (auditory, feeling) of a poem against adjoining works or a wish to create more variety or connection within the section, as much as thematic or formal considerations. I have included a chronological listing at the back of the book for those interested in progress through time and representations from specific volumes. There are also various notes on specific poems for those interested in some background as well as other acknowledgements, where relevant.

This book is not a 'best of'. What I think is 'best' one day, will change with time. My selection approach considered what could be of relevance to an ongoing sense of my work, what poems had been remarked on by readers and critics/reviewers through the years as being of consequence (of course, those opinions have been varied), and what seemed to work when read aloud, to make a reasonably judicious mix of my own approaches to writing. In a few cases, my own emotional attachments to certain poems came into play (though emotional attachment can be self-defeating, and I left out quite a few of those in the end). Unsurprisingly, most of this is a personal reckoning, though those responses from readers and the feel of the read-out poem acknowledge that poems are published and performed out in the world, that poems are social texts, and one's own taste or attachment is not always the best judge, though it clearly plays a part. Of course, another editor would have made a very different selection.

I have also restricted the number of poems chosen from my first four books, up to and including *Screens Jets Heaven: New and Selected Poems*, published in 2002. This very fact, of an earlier new and selected, meant those older books have already had a similar representation once before. I also decided not to include in full any of the longer sequences I have published in various books. This was a pragmatic decision, a function of available space. I have included a few extracts from some sequences, a little reluctantly, but I did want to acknowledge these works in some way, as they have some significance within my broader work. However, I regret I can't offer the complete versions of these, or include other longer poems. I also, in the end, excluded some of the more adventurous or linguistically experimental poems, as this context did not quite suit them and, again, space was an issue.

My approach to writing has never been confined to a particular paradigm. Writing poetry doesn't operate like that, at least for me. On the one hand, the observational has guided much of my writing, some of it quite directly, based on notations made 'on site', so to speak, and sometimes less so. I remember as a kid standing on our back balcony, looking up at the stars or across the small suburban valley where we lived. I realised even then, I was just a small being amongst everything out there. There is, I hope, a sense of those various frequencies of light and sound and other sensual moments throughout my work, that these moments have their mysteries, those things we can't know, or at least I can't. On another hand, a lot of my writing has adopted more experimental approaches to writing, although every poem is an experiment in some sense, the ongoing labour of how to work with language. There are other directions I've also taken, in particular, pushing the lyric past various boundaries.

So, the poems manifest in various ways. Clarity can be as difficult as the linguistically complex. The difficult poem can be rewarding and opens up meanings and feelings continuously. I have gone both ways, sometimes in the same poem. There are many different ways to 'mean'. I am not afraid of metaphor — language is a metaphor — but I'm not wedded to metaphorical flourish or excess, and have at times preferred the associational, the paratactic, chance or formal procedure, or, simply, literal description. The possibilities of the poem are what interest me — form, sound, connotation, address. I want my poems to convey something, at least at the 'how' or 'where' level, if not the more obvious 'what' or 'why'. Sometimes it is quite obvious, of course.

As a result, I realise, and others have said, my work doesn't fit easily into a specific school, category or type of Australian poetry. However, my work isn't written in a vacuum. I write, inescapably, within the contemporary world, and countless influences, including many poetries of now and the past, particularly beyond the Anglophone poetry world, are reflected here in various ways.

Also reflected here are many versions of someone that may be a Jill Jones. But you don't need to know me to get the poems. Many of the poems use the first person, grammatically, but 'I' doesn't belong to any one person. There's no story of my life here, though the words are written out of where I've been, out of experience, and how speech and writing work through an individual.

There are many people who have been very helpful and generous over the many years I've been writing: friends and family, fellow poets, readers, critics, editors, publishers. The list is too long to include here but they know who they are, and I thank them wholeheartedly. I do wish to particularly thank David Musgrave for agreeing to take on this volume and the other folks at Puncher & Wattmann for their fine work on making this happen and their ongoing championing of the broad scope of Australian poetry. Also thanks to Aidan Coleman for offering useful advice on structuring the book. Above all, I wish to thank Annette Willis for support, ideas, forbearance, and most of all, sustaining love.

Jill Jones, February 2023

1.

*I'm on my way under clouds
which don't let anything escape
(you have to deal with it)*

Deliberation on Sudden Days of Exceptional Brightness

These were the lines of our life here
along the street. Cars were all candid
in their leaving. No-one could make a decision.
We meditated on timetables. We thought
about spending wisely, messaging coupons.
We became aware of sirens and strangers
of early flights, all but solitude.

Thought had drugged the music. It was
reduced to interest rates, beautiful soft furnishings
on night programs. Despite the poster's
green outline, it was old politics, tea cups,
amiable kickbacks. Doors closed. There were
only clicks. Poets made words of little boats.
The air could not be still.

Yet, how sanguine the rain became between
the lightning. The sky rhymed with
747s, Cessnas, drones. We were still there
washed in discordant fashion sense.
There was a gulf that didn't allow sleep.
Choices were wrapped in colours of the same size.
It was clear at this stage but inevitably failing.

There were also exceptional bright days
almost as if weather could no longer alarm us.
It was not the time to hate everything.
But not quite the time to dance. We gave up
determining fences. We'd ask, who is my enemy?
Or post, 'Do not abandon these words.'
As if that was the answer.

The Moon, Antares, and the Dead As Well

'The problem of time is like the darkness of the sky'
John Berger, and our faces, my heart, brief as photos

We don't see our faces in the stars, tonight, or any night.
   They're older than faces.
What do we do with the problem of time? I wonder what rivers do.
   Or estuaries, atoms, clouds, constellations, in their time.
All those traces as threads, so even the absent are present.
   The dead as well.
As though there's a perimeter, an edge to the realm-that's-not-us.

Look, there's the past, the crescent moon! And above it Venus
   then Jupiter, and further up the sky, Antares in Scorpius.
The moon's light takes just over a second to reach our faces.
   That light from Antares left itself just before the birth of Galileo.
Always a past touches us, as this hot January forgets us.
   To imagine Galileo on such a night, as if he might
walk here still, looking for ancient heat above this heat.

This pulse of a big, old story is far from our traffic and trees,
   our ground's levels and hollows. We don't hear it.
We can only think and feel into this time, our time
   that remembers the living and 'all-that-the-living-are-not'.
But the dead aren't us.
   Nor are they stars, despite all the names up there.
Someone left a beer bottle next to the street tree.

I hear voices in a yard nearby.
   Who's speaking at this hour, charging the night?
Maybe in the dark, things are more tolerable.
   Maybe in the dark you're not yet born.
Tonight's cold thin moonlight falls onto their faces.

Hear them laughing, not loudly.
Like a conspiracy. Of being with. Maybe together, outside.

Close your eyes and
   keep them open.
Maybe turned upwards into the past,
   or towards me now.
The past as now to come.
   Where we also are in gone light
coming light.

I Walk As Jittery Mortal

I walk out into the curious air.
I trip on matter that's going cold.
I feel earth as thrust, metal and scrape.
I look at each plant for belief or breath.
Their brights unveil me as shadow or guest.

I want to feel a whole lot better than quiet.
I'm singing like a lost chorus of one.
Damp and grit play giddy round my shoes.
I step through it. Nothing quite catches.
Afternoon rain begins its restlessness.

Air is my home. I entered it dripping.
Now here's the jittery earth.
Now here's crust and brown flare
a muster of body for bodies.
Out here I hardly know myself, finally.

Sorrow isn't something I'd name.
It would only sound nostalgic or sappy.
This world isn't mine.
Here I'm a mortal subject.
There are cold things I can't brush away.

Out of These Curves

Each building looks like a letter bending the frame.
It's easy to hide in the curves
where water drips like a song.

The list we kept of daily rainfall had a lot of zeroes.
It's harder to read the sunlight between
hunched floors of the car park.

See this backpack leaning against the wall.
Perhaps it's lost.
Those high ledges give me the blues.

On the bus I concentrate on Dickinson's dashes
and Keats' bad spelling. Sometimes I feel
swayed from language as if avoiding road works.

Sky's beautiful dry shadows fall on my pages
through the familiar spectrum.
All my food's been wrapped in words.

I'm talking with a corrupted document file,
old notes, the spreadsheet I thought I'd lost.
Perpendiculars aren't comforting.

The book I intended to finish is still at home
on the bedside table. Tonight rare rain will drip
like a meticulous dream into the roof cavity.

There's a soft insistent sound in the grevilleas.
Even the yellow door is sighing.
I'm still forming words out of these curves.

Big Apple Leaf Summer

I am to swing, opening gates
a child bearing summer to its end
with the kindness of leaves.
I am to be diamonds, pick-me-ups
queer riddles you do not know.
Not an English evergreen
breaking
but empress of milk
the blood I leave for the ages.

I am to proliferate.
I am roseate and frequent.
I am a sextant. I am full of sky.

I once walked across the playground.
My confusion was greater than the hills.
There was too much bread
and circumstances were not
looking great.

The leaves are my sisters.
We fall.

Edge Against Sign

my life is about letters
against rust around the garden
and weeds at the tips of
your fingers below the horizon beyond
midnight roar for the magic ring
from the poster in the right-hand
pocket into small grottoes of sweet
biscuits like blazes of tourism and
local fashion on a gum leaf

out flat over a small round
table round the side through
shattered glass to rocky outcrops under
freeway pylons up into the
valley with feet with friends with
insects up in the building under
noise towards the open doorway

through the smallest lens round the
lit-up tank over a guitar case
out into universes on the table
of used plates like something i dreamed
into silent gullies drains dumping grounds
in a place in a room in
wires from dark green hollows

for a second down by the harbour
behind its dull red wall at the centre
above a police car at the corner at
edge against sign breaking
being wide awake
after death perhaps

The End of May

The courtyard sounds sloppy with rain.
The sun is there always, but behind darkening clouds.
There's a mess of green and yellow on trees and paving.
It's nearly 11am and still not warmed.
Traffic stutters on North Terrace.
The oak leaves are familiar but wrongly exotic.

Hear all that sound, which isn't the little city
though it chugs and plugs away on slippy streets
but all that sound, as birds gather
lorikeets near sparrows, magpies near turtle doves
all that sound of all those birds all the time
making curves and swathes and jokes of the squares
the city persists into though they don't really work.

I guess all the machines moving are also important
even what I'm doing is probably important, to someone.
It's decisions and numbers, while the ticking of a truck
backing into a space someone wants it to be in
makes it seem fresh and real and busy
inside and outside. Then the bloke in the truck
gets down and has words with another bloke.

I have words too, checking them on pages
as if getting past each line or sentence is something
achieved or, that's right, important.
The men give it up and begin unloading with
that metal sound of purpose and quota.
It's still cold and slippery out in this world.
Still and always full of bird calls.

That the leaves are also shining today.
That there's still a golden sense in greying stonework
of the early twentieth century building
in one corner of the courtyard.
That there's still dust on the plate glass windows opposite
and they never seem to change in any light.
That birds in all this time will sing longer than
the courtyard and the desk, the buildings and the squares.
That this doesn't matter, that it does.

The Quality Of Light

The light comes and goes
like a cloudy day in the 80s
or maybe the 90s, but anyway
a past time, when there were wires
and the incandescent
and a playful sun.
Maybe even an Impressionist
as late as Monet would
recognise it, even as his
eyesight failed during WW1.
Even though he's long dead. But the sun,
the atmosphere, the clouds
I can see, any day I look up, are
there, and changing there
with or without me. With or
without me writing as though
they are there for me.
But I'm not there, in the letters
though I may scribe them
while drinking coffee or watching
turtle doves running along
the top of the fence
as another truck slowly prints out
tyre tracks in the dust along the
new rail's construction corridor.

Ink impregnates paper.
That does not seem remarkable
and it's not, if the words
merely 'come'. Exhaust and clanging
compose the day, as well
as light. And I think the air has become

more opaque since the 90s, though it's still
full of movement, of wings
and sound, water, leaves, disgorgement.
In the bird bath there's a yellow leaf
clearer than in the ponds, I presume,
of Giverny, only 80k from Paris
but a place I've never been, or
the nerve system of creeks leading into
the Torrens, or the oily wash
of Sydney Harbour.
Luminosity perhaps is a dream,
like travel, building, or words. It all
comes and goes, it is
as if it's happening, at least
that's the impression, like light
as so much fails.

Bitumen Time

When you go home in dark,
when the street sings, bitumen thing,
or you, yourself, sing
this like birds, this like moths, don't
let anyone sing it for you
or anyone tell you, other than
this is whatever you make in the dark,
wherever you take this in the morning, because
there were things felt, times, places,
minutes that knocked, 'things that did not matter',
they do, of course, they do,
sounds that curve, drift down the long dark, a type
of sky song, hardness, cement walk, where
you trip, where the roses are stripped
of winter colour, indeed, who am I among
scent of this night flowering in dead arms of winter, so,
who can compare me, who softens me, is it
like childhood, as though history ramps into
the moon's famous indifference, the sky's
night version of real things that hold into
strange corners, so help me, help me,
it's transparent, but so alien, all these stories
I'm told before time rushes on
covering its angles.

Wrack

which way are you facing as the street falls
trees burst, windows crack
the rust has no consciousness but it attacks
a load of pipes crashes from the roof rack
of the white car scraping the wall
out the back, pink balloons bounce
on each other like feral boobs doing that dance
to attract an exchange of cash, love, consumption
it's a gasgaspgrasp, and an old woman is aghast
staring up at the hills where the horizon's
gone black and the wind makes that evil dash
through your soul's soul, what is it? Mars attacks?
it's all brooding wrack or media flack, the rain
that never rains will rain and no attempt at
political hack will stop the weathering of weather
the tide comes, it's not going back

The Beautiful Anxiety

The paths are full of iron and stars.
Who does not welcome all this
black, burning with misplaced rain?
If it's reported that islands have gone
missing, remember how seas love us
and trail in our blood.
If there's too much of a ghost now
upon the clouds, a wing, a roar
none of that will open
the dead to this world again.

There's nothing purely accidental
in your edgy condition.
Damage seems almost a necessity.
If there's beauty in patina, it's here
not just waiting for the cracks
in the permanent. It's subcutaneous
like a language that entered you
without stamps of approval.

You step out with your necessity
because nothing will grow within
houses for too long.
Your sandals and heels, your capped toes
they are some kind of assurance
along with the belated rain, whose water
slaps the ridges of your song.

Each tree that wasn't there before
each element or fibre, the occasional feather
or slip of whitened excrement
the glassy tips of plastic that flutter

as you pass, they are places.
Hands have admitted them
and their appearances
have depended on each isobar and swell
of time zones.

You must be going elsewhere
see how it skews the horizon and adds
something green to the temperature.
There are instruments for this
kind of knowing, along with bright machines
moving tonnage along temporary roads.

But if you can still turn your hand around
the rain and touch skin's rearranging
of its walking —

figures
atoms
curves
droplets

and distinguish the cold of it, dropt on
sun shadows within the petrochemical hum
it's erotic scent, a ghost of ash
passing stars, and a kind of subliminal speech
among legends of flowers and birds, roses
of the place where the phoenix plays
that useless search within the art of speech
to fly amongst lost things again
the long road from the north
hard sails built out of trawl.

There's never time to know
yourself. That's the beautiful anxiety
of moving, as each gutter, each wing
each clip, or semiconductor
the air dripping through your skeleton
your fur that scares easily, as it all
seems to be crashing.

The air moves history into history.
You look where leaves hold the light
skin holds the light
edges hold the light.

Nothing holds on
the light.

Wave

The traffic begins its wave,
the sky is threaded with exhaust,
the blind man has a ticket, your bag
is heavy today, the traffic is beautiful
going somewhere, the sky does not move
though it seems to, the hours begin
to waver, you begin to think of effort
and time, the endless hatcheries
of capital, the blind man knows the way,
the traffic is heavy with somewhere,
the sky is beautiful though
it doesn't seem so, the hours thread
with tickets or numbers.
The numbers are beautiful,
rolling along like waves.
And in afternoon the blind man
waits with you, the sky is endless
but it is not, the traffic is threaded
with numbers, each ticket is beautiful
within its own exhaust.

Misinterpretations /or The Dark Grey Outline

I move through a slanting,
footpaths erupting roots through bricks
near the mad old bus stop.
I used to know what I was thinking,
now it's a field, inside,
is it green, or grey water, horsing,
gridding, heavens bent
through the fleck.
Sometimes I wonder if I'm drinking the wrong water,
the other day I read
I had a sort of degree, but I ain't, no way Hose-Bloody-Zay.
Please, I-am-not-a-doctor,
I'm too unfashionable for that.

Even in Sydney
when days get cuter than cop cars,
as the city train smells of its electricity and cut-up vinyl,
makes you want to chisel rocks with letters,
makes you think, placing As while breathing
Hawkesbury sandstone,
oh gritty gritty something,
don't let go.

But from Greenhill Road I can see a Dark Grey Outline,
gums on the Toorak Gardens horizon
after rain pins on Portrush,
windy,
juggle juggle,
that's the bus tyres.

Tickets are eaten,
baskets savaged, cars dinking in line.

It seems average but sounds pushy
out the window,
my eyes scram down choosing the wet leaf
blown onto a white roundabout.
Something I learned when I was young,
shape is serious matter.
I am not what I'm supposed to be.
Light is spring silver
and escapes my language,
in the next lane
'fragile goods'.

Outside a North Terrace carpark
is the Ha-Ha Arrow,
pointing white blue charge grips,
tinker tinker bus blows money,
odd jangles of student housing,
arrivals not quite fusion (Go Backwards).

The second lift won't stop
at the fifth floor,
'it's worth reporting'. What, corridors?
In here, it's ice white as carpet,
closing time.
If you don't approve,
or burn, 'therefore'.
Perhaps I am Missing Pages Out Of My Life.
I've always been flaky, lost and shaky,
but never 'ponderous' over my territory,
that takes planning.
It's always been weather not
geosophy (that's so fashionable! yeah?).
I'm delicate, sandy,
unknown, please, or 'to not know',

falling without finding.

But what am I thinking, of giving up the desk,
going off-road, gravelling, dirt thrash?
Why not, given the green's mixed up,
weather rattled, promises running off
leaves as prediction pouring through vents.

The creeks are high,
snake tongues, feathers,
water calls, absolutely
and briefly,
tomorrow forks
but for now
full cold moon
and wrestling night.

I have dreamed green tiles,
walls, gaps, dirty grassy
penalty signs,
curves, yes, finally,
pink ankle
and all this air, all this.

If I'm not what I'm supposed to be
then why all this certainty,
how do I escape its cackling old Sprache?

Night in Frome Road
is there at its hour,
cold erupting through asphalt,
sight and feeling mashed with
my flaking alphabets.

Marrickville Sonnet

Per mezz'i boschi inhospiti et selvaggi
onde vanno a gran rischio uomini at arme
  Petrarch, Sonnet No. 176

But to learn all there is in a street.
To treat the suburb's noise as another lesson.
The amazement of traffic. Or celebrate
small terrors that balloon from locks and veins.
O industry, garden, railway, brothel!
grafted on sandstone hill and bushland.
Where, once, a clean slow winding river.
A sacred kingfisher rests in my backyard.

Main street clogs, a continual bloodline.
Shopping hearts work with speed, decay.
Young maestros repair wheels at pools of oil.
Stabs of music hurl across the street,
infuse my lines with deep bass notes.
As if heaven lies about us. Or love is brief.

Train in Vain

The blue is vast and hot
  where is it taking us?

We, to be somewhere
  the platform, smoking summer.

The door swings only one way this time
  the writer was beaten by the past.

There is no driver on the train
  it is safe to travel.
Did the voice say that?

It's a long climb to the outside
  mind the oleanders — save your children.

The air is sliced
  we would welcome it.

He is full of blue jeans
  there are those who would welcome it.

It's the metal that stings
  but you could argue about the high rise.

There's a little bleed in the cutting
  it goes brick by brick by brick.

There's nothing to be sought
  you won't come to anyway.

Yellow ribbons in her hair
how excited can we get?

The Institute is red
the face of time is silver.

Museum, its brass, the past
we rush through underground.

If there are no exceptions to all of this
please stand closer.

in the distance on the verandah

having said yes too many times and become loaded,
i believe you, 'all doors lead to busy rooms',
the darkness can roll in while you're not looking
so afternoon sprouts night outside your window
when you were turned away by talk and didn't notice,
they say you can't predict the tide accurately,
or turn back the future, but the phone is continuous,
and it occurs to me
i have moved from being just a prisoner
to a more debatable shadowland
within which i'm circling but not holding
or closing,
at lunch she talks about the void, she's seen it,
i know what she means, over wine and smorgasbord i try
to remember to say my name,
overhearing the man next me: 'we know where we're going now',
and i lift my quiet glass to him, wondering who we are, later,
walking down my path, i expect to meet myself
hanging around the front door,
a drifter on the verandah, pale face and misleading eyes,
or sometimes i look up and see someone just like me
poring over the distance at the edge of the balcony
tracing where i've been: in streets, in rows, on the way
to another trial, another room, another meeting,
having said yes once again, and misplaced something

mother i am waiting now to tell you

mother about the letters i never wrote
                        the sirens outside batter my heart
and the fact i don't eat enough food
                        reminding me that i am hungry
all that heavy seductive stuff
                        in the nights of new traffic in dreams
and i do not understand your eyes
                        where there is so much blindness
the glare of your tenacity almost breathing
                        i am struck down at the window
i have prayed to be that strong — resisting also
                    the death squads are squealing in the backyards
but there is too much noise — two languages now
                    spray painting their names like manifestoes
like what you wanted me to be — like this
                    i don't like the sound my fear makes
and like someone else who has my voice
                    i talk to myself — begging that someone
who has my arms but speaks a different love
                    will remember the answer to the enigma
which you have lost the words for
                    i am waiting for them to tell me
i am waiting now to tell you

Jazz and Stars

The jazz of the morning plays between slats

A piece of cellophane winks at noon

Clouds cast over the west in the evening

Scraps of stars fall in a backyard

Children open their eyes on the quiet

This Crumbling Aura

There's nothing sacred about me. I was born under stars
that kept moving. Outside I could smell lost temperatures
stolen dust   my blood tainted with history.
But here I am without a prayer   looking for gods in everything
that's melting. I watch the littlest sparrow. It knows
where the crumbs are.

I broke marriage. I never fitted shoes. And where would I walk?
In the dark men will kill you   and in scuzzy city light as well.
I'm never better than in some unknown country
called a dream   though even there men kill me.

And even here I wake up in my own breath, the only thing
I've given back, scuzzy, scared   tainted   nothing holy
even in the way I walk past seats and palms   where girls
look like Debbie Harry or Chrissie Amphlett   in songs out of
another time, a virtual place   my local understanding
shimmering along my skin   as an iffy aura, a rapture, pleasure
and pain.

All I am is a jump cut, montage   a fiction to myself
in my profane air, badly edited   but knowing where the crumbs are.
I'm inhabited by stories, fevers, voices and lies   heaving
this breathing into light that changes every moment. There's no way
to rescue me, even as a translation of an original hymn.
Am I simply my little secret?

Sometimes the dark is just the way a room is
or that part of a blink   that flicker of closing.

Maria Callas is With Me Tonight

Maria Callas is with me tonight,
broadcasting from her stage of heaven.
She glides me over city roads glittering
black light after rain.
She waits with me in my head at the bus stop,
fills my sky from 1954 to forever.
I soar onto the bus but no-one looks.
A spring moth turns and turns crazy,
topgunning the ceiling of the bus,
but Maria doesn't notice,
her priestess jealousy grips my head
fiercer than the headphones,
or the bus lurching into my stop.
It's a love I want to understand.

As I cross for home, the last short leg,
boys crowd the footpath, yelling,
the girls watch, edging each other.
They all look up at me
as the lights turn orange.
Is this the end?
Will Norma die while I get rolled?
Maria Callas is still with me tonight.
I stride out over this last road
that's cold, smelling of more rain,
danger coursing through my head.
The kids regroup, ignoring me,
and Maria and I stroll down the hill
with my heaven she's visiting tonight.
I'll live happy there, happy as I can be
without love I understand.
She's got one more scene to play.

The Skim

Warnings that I walk through
the hassle at the station
the boredom at the counter
chill before I step down.

The day that is saturated
the harbour that is bruised
wavelands of graffiti
and movements of poetry.

The urging and the following
the exceptions and excuses
knuckles in the pockets
and the yellow curse.

Tunnels that enclose
the languages we swallow
the return that I wait for
whoever got there first.

Windows that are flying
the street that rises slowly
rain shine I walk through
blue breaking up the clouds.

The safety that I pray for
the water of thy skin.

from Where We Live

1. Scratchings, Rust

Heaven, if you look up, isn't black as it used to be. Our window is a prayer, and beyond, the line a day makes. We look out one morning into the way of streets, amongst magpie scurf, chasing bird mind.

Each scratch a water history.

The clear could be
what we're waiting for.
Or we search
for different evidence
equal to
the same odd beauty
that's more
than distraction.

A canvas of anxiety
inscribes walls
and metal
where birds
and people go over
paving and crossings.

Much is overwritten.
Much disappears in
telling the hours.

window beyond makes scratch
waiting beauty
walls birds over

6. Demolition, Window

We come together over the way of an image, the way of our streets, the way we walk it. Leaves and shadows hang on the wall, stand out somehow without saying a word. I don't know all these languages but they are about love. Take my hand into it.

These are the hymns.

A canvas of anxiety
The guano of ages
A pattern of wings
The way of our streets

The brilliance of words
Bones of the neighbourhood
Loops of existence
A flutter of rain

For what we are
For what we take
For what we have
For what we make

Signs weave amongst
the wonderful dust
and absences assigned by words
the present days and skies.

Voices out of other times.
Crumpled shores.
All the things you might want.

Then realities break into each other.
Then there's an instant, a syllable of light.

This is how it is sung.

shadows into signs
dust absences
voices
might break light

The Make-Do

The day drops voices
on my tongue, all the burnt dust,
garbage, tenderness. Duties waste time.

I am stupid among crisp brown leaves.
I lick salt fresh from the window
and wait for the big moon.

I get more curious than you think.
Change is impure, vulgar,
a magnificent rush in make-do.

Dust sticks to my daydream shoes.
A taxi revs its autonomy and escapes
into a dirty, unclear horizon.

The main road is a dream hatched,
a tremendous streaking
in the fast fold of fret lines.

I can't always dash moments.
I haunt my junk.

The Spare Winter

Each week the weather spirals
cold on the rails. The blue falls.
I've pinned hopes on a ticket away
closed my door on the Snowy winds.
The camellia gave up two flowers, alone
I write myself into mystery at the window.
I gather simpler things on the plate
and count the birds I've missed in the strife.

Each day tendencies breach headphones
no-one sits among silence.
In deep city thralls there's a kind of happiness
at each counter something ordinary and bright.
'Praise and blame belong to youth and glory.'
Even a pair of sneakers grows old quick.
Winter rain can almost manage its balm
the black cat softens the iron roof.

A Moon Song

Sometimes the town needs to be silent
Let its secret crows sing, however
They carry changes

The moon's white eye closes on the horizon
Leaves accompany us along the road
My fingers feel out the cold on the gate

There's more night now and perhaps more time

2.

It is impossible to live as if we are free

Whose Words Did These Things?

Whose workbenches made these thirsts
pounding out like stereos, stiffening
the air-conditioner? Who can tell
when you're lonely?
But we'll survive wisecracks and wishbones
or loaf amongst the dead of the crossroads,
the proof to which we are not entitled.

There's an expansion of sinew containing
the freewheeling we undergo;
loosening our gymslips we turn on kaleidoscopes
then watch our hands as the similarity electric
charges dryness — but we are not static
and we are not grief, but fill
our hands with the spill and as it fizzles
it frets and comes fullest 'til it breasts
yes, you know how it breaches anew though
it's old, much older than workbooks.

But breathe and merge, then lug down words
don't pussyfoot round the sidelines. And if
you die a little here, you might embrace the wrench
and relish workdays again.

Brilliant Slippy Works

They took all my money.
I earnt that money
scraping rancid face cream
from pink containers
to be recycled as mouth wash, or icing.
That wasn't my issue.
I could almost taste the cream
and the brilliance of the plastic.
That wasn't my concern.
The fence next door was weak
where the beige cat entered.
The cat stole our sandwiches
from the lunch room.
The light stole my eyes and I did not want
to recover them until pay day.
The envelopes were full of soap powder.
That was the next job
cat detergent, but it was not my problem
though the union rep was slack.
We smelt his beige ambition.
The light entered my head through
my remaining follicles.
I slipped on the cream.
I could make a case out of that.
The cat was sick in the urinal
well, thank heaven for that
it was not my responsibility.
I put my bag down for two seconds
and, voila, it was gone.
How did they do that?
I was not in the light but
it was no longer my conundrum.

My elbow's still sore from when
I slipped on the face cream.
The cat knows its brilliance.

Blue Lines

It's not the birds that are spectres,
they come in afternoon, true,
swing by the air, song-filled passes,
that branches come to ground, falling
with dryness and shadows, remembering
midnights rather than afternoons,
declining drugs rather than passing shots
to make shadows in the lens that swings
the casual reach through spectacle
of shadows on a dance floor and wings
flashing off drags, or you, queer bird,
dropping each sequence twisting in and out
of presence, the dry air that falls like a truism
once you've left the afternoon filling
its own spectre of west light and husks
of autumn that birds let fall, that grounds
fill as fallen, dance for earthed shadows,
the passing sequence husked with
casual twists of a lens through its stops
as if the machinery could drag light back
again, dancing jewels, red and green feathers
flashing a pass, a queer shot the sun's moment
holds, not yet declining.

The Phantom Division

They're restructuring reality again
but you have to sit and wait your turn
the transfers have been coming down for weeks
and another truckload of files
is settling into the archives
there's a floating field of rumour
closer to the truth than all the press releases
sounds of a makeshift power struggle
flood out into corridors
with eviction notices for the defeated
you lose your harbour views and your identity
you consider a career in espionage, lunch or motherhood
you are now dependent on radar
as unit after unit cuts out
you dream of limbo, you dream of voodoo
and pray they will take you at dawn instead
and shoot you full of silence
falling under the noise
of statutes, photocopiers and ministerial privilege
you want to believe fervently
that it has nothing to do with you
but you begin to learn the spell-cast anyway
how to reconstruct phantoms
you send away for the magic ring
you begin to use the telephone
you start to get in touch.

Patience Without Virtue

Everyone loves the female voice.
Am I forgiven for having one?
I wait patiently, hoping it's only
to do with simple flowers. It never is.

I dissent again, the moon goes as it came.
There's nothing transcendental within reach.
What must I do amongst sweat
grey flannel, car parks, and theories?

I can only be a certain kind of lunatic
and women are vaster than history.
It's the way I don't step forward politely.
No point sitting on the fence.

It's the way I have to fix things
by painting a sign. 'I can't believe
I still have to protest this fucking shit.'
I can't put the leaves back.

My affinity is always a question.
I can't recall when these things didn't happen
in my cells or beaten-up memories.
I'll never be as dead as a man.

Blue

We are thinking the unthinkable today
as if we can't describe the truth.
We are almost outside the building.
We've found success in an obstacle
but what if nobody knew
there is nothing outside language
except for this deep blue sky.
We are not outside the building.
There's controversy over the timing of data.
Our staff were trying to hide something
so there's nothing outside blue.
We were reviewing our core ceremonies.
Someone hid excuses in a desk.
We're almost inside a colour like blue.
They're crashing answers on tarmac
while we stand on this platform of pledges
painted azure and normal.
We have a hit list of reductions.
There's nothing outside outside.
We've introduced some powerful nostalgias.
We stand near proud in our self-embellishment.
Indeed amplitude is a hurdle.
We stand with almost nothing deep in blue skies.
This is our final and vital lie.

Email is a Record

It says it all in the corridor, 'please,
give me a break'. Here are the excuses
faces turning red in the plasma, (we're all
mates) while outside, chemical rain
nodding blow-up dolls, dozens of thrusting
microphones, and the trawlermen, partake
of the delay, the short-lived scandals, while
the poles keep melting.
     You stop your hand at a keystroke
wondering about the reply you'd need to make
ascending the high moral ground, staking
a claim on another new minister. Give me
a break, each minute is something you create
the trees in the parklands are dying
every email's a fake.

The Vertigo Blues

My aura quivers with fall. The maple's yellow paper blows
through the front door in veiny stanzas like ink crackling.
What is true? The camellia opens its white heart slowly. I wear
these blues like spread-out night. All pianists talk to their keys.

I disturb skinks with water. The oboist dances on a
column of air. There's something shivery at the threshold.
A saxophone edges out tracks inside the machine.
The old dog brushes the passage next door. Outside
a phone rings 'hello' in Jay-Z or Wolfmother, something
from Brahms that won't let me sleep. The world is loose.
Ghosts are barking, even cats shimmer.

The stage is set for rain, but sky shakes the blood, shakes
every note. And thought, that diamond, has again
been released. Yet, all my bent cheques, the sanity
of white tea, my unused sleep, my lost amulets, have not
been wasted. What makes it so difficult is also what
keeps me here, still. There are silhouettes above
my heart, a brace of baggy riffs two-timing below.

In the shining trumpet of night rain, I realize this climb
will get harder and harder and not like heaven, that
it's benign to fall. How it seems, is how it happens. How
earth moves. All is so beautiful and shifting terribly.

O Fortuna

At times you're like a *machiavellista* planning to meet
whatever culminations you wish to thwart
on a Friday — well, it's nearly the weekend, the trees
are full of lorikeets and despite rain's desultory patter,
there's a fuzzy window of blue sky coming
from the south, wholly unexpected, the weather's governance
being a method above you. We all have our fortuna
we pretend we've never met, there's no point
in deception here unless it's your art. There's a timetable
dissembling just before the weekend, the doors of the end
carriage won't open as the train pulls up,
someone's limping under a backpack, you recall
your own blemishes. It's that 'tragic sense of life'
yukking around between faith and reason, the mortal
combat. While you work hard for the money, you want
to grab a towel and the 30+, hie yourself to the plage
dodging pale hooligans and melanoma. Surely
the end is nigh and it's a faith squeeze, when to be
heterodox, when to hold the line, which comes at you
up front and always, always leaves you past, belated,
but still humid with life at the turnstyles pushing
another weekly into the slot, watching it burst
up again. While folding your damp umbrella
into these sharp hectic hours, you keep appearing.

All Night, All Night

Under erratic stars and sirens
raising us out of our beds,
the emergencies, the virus spreads,
how it ends, like a story,
who knows, through the grids,
through the planet's ways,
under the sway of the dark lit
with passages, the lake fills
far north, the planes bring in
more of those a-dying, we are
filled with facts, queries, nothing
so certain as each one's fear,
what will befall, what will all this
become, a plague of our making
or something we would rather not
done, but rise above the plain, ancient
in misery to find a place, divest
the hurt, who knows
what has ultimately been undone
under polypropylene, bad miming
of the original sung coasts, swarms
of blue fish, the white, the green,
the real schools so long
for the learning, underneath clouds,
but still, now, the sirens squealing,
and we must hurry along
in our caring, these bodies of ours,
kiss them while the world
is tearing, all night, tears all night
from the north and from the gulf
into here, past here, who will ask
where it comes from?

Sorry I'm Late

The snow was in the sun
There was a prick in the garden
A truck jack-knifed the particulars
There was a smell of old gas
The crows lost
As did the roses and all that juice we spilled for love
That prick in the garden

Photographers were lighting bombs
The olive tree fell just as we were getting started
We forgot to fill out the form
Celebrity drug disasters were drifting in our channel
My watch shows tomorrow's date
The disk shattered
There's that smell again
It's a form of expediency, or is it complexity?

I tried to inform the authorities

If I could find my name and my reason
If the birds would stop drifting like that
If someone would lend a hand at the entrance
I'd be less nervous saying this
My throat would work with my head and hands

Mystery Train

The things you try
when you're 18
leaving nothing behind
so beautiful as 1956
a bell-hop's hat
ghost of a morning's love
in a river city
mysterious travellers
with, maybe, a .38
riding round all night
everyone looks like Elvis

— refers to scenes in the Jim Jarmusch film of the same name

All Blues

You tried to explain it to the cop
and he knew you were hurting
there's something about the grey walls
a hint of blue, watery, and insubstantial
alibis or security, we're all
dumb fucks as far as that goes
here the young officers all look like dykes
even the women, it's that blue again
all blues, and people sniffing the desk
hello darkness, but that's crap, the light
is generous and mean at once, so long as
you don't have to sign anything, and hope
you don't turn up in the mug shots
covered in plastic, needing a makeover
stop nodding your head, this will go on
all night around the dirty lilac seat
frozen moments, well, you've had enough
of those but that's better than a purpose
or the wherewithal. He sees you
and that's weirdest of all. At least there's
nothing green in here.

A Time To Refrain From Embracing

If you fear light or the dark tree
the root at your feet, if you step badly
your arms grow lame wings
dull and hard, before the sudden man
with elliptical transports, as
dust will rise, coagulate like stone, as
his pummel rounds on you
you will go down, depart your usual
height and air, your old agreement
his steel line, your cotton square shoulders
gutter is not excited by the stars
you fold onto world floor
and, yes, it's grit, your drift, now
he'll open your arms, your legs, now
attempt, extract, your sky blue pocket
his teeth will close upon any words
escape or thrill, 'take me in your arms'
he will not please you, your dry breath
his mighty need, his hidden tongue
you will fist pavement, crush footpath
gasp into ground feet, trees
where it all grows and dies
you carrion, you clung, diamond thought
hardens night, lithic and gleaming
your breast bone, your elbow
grips sentences, holds all words
let just one song, leaf bird, the arrow
what will fly, unheard, that cries
he is the dog, you do not play
he is the wall, you do not wear out
in the lifted wail he loses faith
swift empty, far gone, night dew, lightning

shadows and spray, you spit stone
speak deep air, throat rattle stings
one street on home.

The Pure in Heart

They have taken babies
and blamed it on dingoes.
They've planted foul words
on the righteous tongues
of six-year old bigots.

They have joined hands
with the makers
of warheads, purification
and sub-Arctic famines.

They have studied love
and found it wanting.

They have flushed their water
through cataracts of ice.
They praise the numbers
in their heavy books.

Some of them watch you,
monitor your garbage
for glimpses of hell.
Be careful, they think
their destiny is to drink
from your children.

The Kitchen Light

If the past is correct, it was here she couldn't move.
They agreed on shadows, let dust slope across the light,
buried watches under the bricks where the damp rose.

Let it be sung! About gravities that pull you down, the sinister
curve of minutes tangling any recall of the point of an argument.
Even the spirits of place had gone, leaving their bottles.

The sounds of doves, more gentle than bruises,
pattered the iron, the rust. The path's slippery green
led from the light of day past cold blue hydrangeas.

When it got beyond even the curiously patterned logic
of their life, all he could swear at was her name.
Though it was not all he hit her with, as she stood.

At this time she could not turn, either this shabby fortune
or the other key, for the new highway. There was no cure
for a pattern of knuckles and fear blooming through skin.

This was their city. It escaped the high beam of summer,
but found among winter's musty shawls, exacting formations
of the cold. She'd trace them in afternoon on grimy glass.

Between battles all her reasons lined up, ready to go.
Breathing a smell of waves, and a mother wrapping up the night
in a kitchen where the big light lived, her room of light.

The Mini Series

Dads play with old train sets —
'it wouldn't kill you to be nice'.

On the soft beach
when there's no surf.

It's the little things you do
for five per cent deposit.

The bar is empty
send them home to their wives.

The violinist has abandoned
the orchestra, the pits.

Stepping into the great southern ocean
no preservatives, all natural.

Saints on TV
when tomorrow is another day.

The lovebirds should be fun
the actor is now far too old.

The steam age has returned
get the baby and the billy can.

Rates are fixed for six months
but you better finish your beer.

'We'll all die using pills.'
We ride the white horses.

I cannot accept that
the dollar is steady.

Refrains on Sand

Because I don't belong here — being from the State of Flux —
my papers do not rhyme.

Because I don't belong here I am living on dust.

Because I don't belong here I have rewritten the sun in all my
dream books. I make up the world each morning and shake
down its streets with the slippery white sand of paradise.

Because I don't belong here I am washed away in forgetfulness
swaying in trees with bats under the pointers of the cross.

When they took me to the train it was the stagnant express.

When I stole the bread they offered me no other choice.

When they disposed of me it was a spark above my head.

When I tried to tell my story they bound my fingers to my heart.

I see my wife on the tender pillow of morning.
I see my husband in every dancing scheme of night.
I see my lover in a grain of sand.
I hear the crocodiles in the hall.

Because I don't belong here I buried my lute and drum. For ten
thousand years you will hear this song as it rises through rocks
thrown on the lips of ground.

Because I don't belong here I recognise the sunken islands of elsewhere and I make the escape of the turtle.

Because I don't belong here my suit is sharper, my hat brim is tight.

Because I don't belong here I have rigged the cannon and pissed on the powder.

Because I don't belong here I do not look like myself and it makes the platforms   anxious.

Because I don't belong here I know it is better and I know it is worse.

Displacements
— a week of conversations

Every day is impossible
I struggle with the outline.

My skyline still breathes, white haze
so close, such distance.

You ring me ... a fortress or a party?
Your brittle joke ... as if we could decide.

Gutturals, street rhythms
the slippery glab of stones in mouths.

Dusty trees shiver in dark
strafed by day, waiting for it to happen.

The prophets of the morning
tag and count in other cities.

Silver clouds, heights and tiny cracks
craters in the midst, holes made by language.

Here we wait, rain clouds, offshore breeze
another boat is sighted.

We are not one, these streets —
but we are many — stones, underground.

We were talking ... speaking ...
or listening to what — the nag of posterity?

We enter ... the stages

where each word will be stolen.

You are packing the jeep, deep
heading for the pale yellow distance.

Never the sum of our parts
we continue drafting other selves.

This cruel movie deal topples —
we die in rehearsal.

I still see us — lounge lizards in the wastes
drinking the green liquor of lost time.

This time ...
Elvis has left the building.

God bless the veil
of dust.

Sydney, September 2001

from Struggle and Radiance: Ten Commentaries

Driving Night Out

In suits, corners
on white-tie boulevard.

You pray for the barbarians
their knowledge, their verse
their surety of wild horses.

O the angst of insurance and facial hair!
O the desire for it all meaning nothing!
The zero within the frame.

Dealers and bouffant guys
fuck wheels
with drink and our lip gloss lies.

White necessity
in the caves
the heart

the passages of eyes.

What's Coming Next

We are coughing because the train is late.
Someone still wears a volunteer's uniform.

The tabloids have all had coupons torn from them.
Maybe it's easier to focus on cloudy days.

No use worrying, the results are in.
Do dreams stand up in the slashing gravel?

An expensive perfume arises out of damp air.
There's the smell of a fire sale.

An age is coming of slow intrinsic diseases.
No matter how long he stares at the map, the carriage falters.

What worked then and what's working now?
Equivalence is in the magic.

In the glass is another world.
You can bare silence and find it neither golden nor clear.

If today is streaky, tomorrow will be unreasonable.
There's a long street where leaves are tipped red.

The peace gets more anxious.
'For sale' signs are out, stapled on plywood.

All bets are off.
You have to go through it.

Pages of legal clauses have upset the momentum of speech.
Functionaries run towards the rain with buckets.

from My Ruined Lyrics

2. I'm Coming

I can't give you any more
although the weir overflows

And here in my pockets
another flow

Of cellophane, an old musket
a slide rule, seed catalogues, powers

The river rises
in the hundred year flood

There's something planetary
in the moan of levees

I lay my hands on
evidence changing gears

My logbook is full of
sneaky miles

The lie is of the tongue

And I would kiss you with it
when I come

The Doll And Me

I hate the doll, its plumpy head,
its brunette swirls, its itsy cheeks,
its pout, its lashes, the uptight clothes,
marrowless arms, nerveless teeth,
its squeaking, the mess
it makes on the floor.
I want to detach the twee wee feet
and hammer it to the fence, drown it,
skewer it to the door, to say 'this is what
has become of us'. Even naked
it makes me angry and afraid.

What if the doll grows? What if
it wants to take me home?
What if the doll ships are waiting,
doll planes, neverending
pink clouds and puffy oceans?
What if the doll says 'I could begin
to take you apart', and
pins a dress to my hollows,
paints me so I smile
at every beastly, devouring kiss.

No, no, no! I must throw it into
the ecstatic sky. Hook it to a comet.
Just like all the monsters,
in their filthy skirts, who says
it can't crash and burn in
rapt and stupefying bliss?

from Six Temperamental Sonnets

6. Finally, Whispers!

With just a little science we can disturb much
in the time-space continuum
if you stay beautiful, and I'm steady, game
in the gravel — rendered from loneliness
my world pushes its conundrums, worming
clarity, dumb intelligence, animal feeling.

Do you remember how it felt after
the motion, or the mediation? Will it be
the goods or their absence, massive temperatures
between thighs, oceans and hot abdomens
sarin gas, river fevers, flash memory, girlie flush.
It's guts, glory, then we're famished, o tasted and gone!

Diversions, combustions, the changa-chang
everywhere! White teeth, sloppy kisses. Such words!

The Louder Silence

Shade is a kind of writing, as well as a kind of light.
It passes across the ceiling well after sundown.
A bird lands on the roof, making that racket again
which spooked everyone last week.

Something crosses our path from the back of the house.
We'd feel uneasy if we weren't so tired.

I swallow water mixed with a solution of mineral grit,
as though it's a cure. As I tip away dregs, the colder night
pours more water from an ugly tap onto my wrist.

The window is still open and shadows blow in
like diesel and roses. The bird takes off, clattering as it goes.
Then a louder silence roars around the moon.
Will it rain?

The shade is full of itself and nothing. The tap still drips.
I get up an hour later to turn it off. The ceiling is clear.

There's an owl somewhere near and a goods train
on the other line. It's scary when it's calm.
Where do you put morning?

Dust and Ice

They're putting insects on film and that obsesses you
nameless nips in the kitchen as the house cracks.

Weirder than wisdom poison enters you, but you
do not go crazy, you do not die.

The sun is unlike silence though it seems white as silence.
No silence is what sings your own sluices.

If you fancy moonbeams, they too are there
clear as a cross above tiles. What carries in the cold air?

Crickets are dying on pathways. Dust and ice mixes
while freight rolls west. The timetable is cracking too.

Toxins don't make you see, if there's no more to sully.
Try learning to dissolve with the crust outside.

Shiver

The cool ether
encourages movement.
You even shiver,
that's unusual now.

Remember to look at
the galaxy
remember to be kind
to leaves, they can't
always be green
and fragrant.

Growing
is hard, there's pain
in all cells.

Blossom

Smell the sky like a hurt
blossom gone to ground.

The displacements make a song
of wrenching.
It's angry, air in the trees.

Even stars dither in the faraway.
The difficulties go on for hours.
The place quivers.

And harm in all its nuances
sings.

Tracking

All the wild dogs
have left the street
empty as the sun
they were dreaming
before the winter came
they set off for the hills
that's where the voices
retain them
above all

even so
they will not
leave me alone

3.

clear, grey light falls forever,
over the other side — the horizon

In My Shifts

I come in with language
I come out of.
Its weed, its shrill bugs.
A harvest, a rot, a dervish.
Cooked into night.
Swum from beginnings.
Patterns at the bottom of a pool.
Something that doesn't fit.
That shifts and fills
my face with stone air
sweet fetid sound
or I sit down with it.

If it feeds me or anyone.
Perhaps with the birds.
Perhaps with imprecation.
Perhaps with what
the sun and rains
tell me, perhaps today.
With my feet muttering.
With technique and nurture.
And my hand that allows
me to come
in with language
then without.

Our Epic Want

It wasn't in the sound of trees or boom-gates.
They'd been burned. The juice had cracked.

Our clothes became tighter. They were black and blue or shot in red,
    infra-red.
It had become a virtual lucky dip, but no love.

You couldn't bet on it anymore, not even on the lam or off shore.
We'd dialled it up but we'd forgotten the hands, their pink skin allure.

We were somewhere in the torn fabric, parting the seams.
We'd given up on claustrophobia.

Raw music stunned us, it hurt more than love.
Did it have cult status? Would we make a hash of it?

There were lists making it official but we weren't on them.
We thought we were owed but we couldn't find the candles or the gun.

There was no meat raffle, no magic jumping castle.
Someone had done the old switcheroo, they said.

We looked up flues and into blowholes.
We found a world of foam and fug and acetylene.

The rain rattled us but it was the wrong size, too big, too grey.
There was nothing between it like love or even its simulacra.

We'd disposed of our means, where was our famous attention to detail?
It wasn't in our helmets.

We'd botched it, we thought, though the dials worked.
We had all the gear in the back, the bogus green passports.

We remembered the abstractions in the boot, they'd crushed the
          mushrooms.
The result looked like omelette or autumn leaves.

There were azure clouds but it didn't smell right.
We expected immunity but it didn't come.

It seemed almost effortless in the end.
We felt a rush.

This wasn't tactics anymore, neither was it pure.
We bought a geiger counter at a garage sale, which blew our minds
          for a while.

We felt good but a little flakey.
Esperanto was no good at all, nor Urdu, nor English.

We could have been in a novel by some Russian.
We're idiots, babe. That old song. We sat in the backyard and it sang us.

We walked down the street. We saw a dog. Some fallen oranges.
The train passed us. We'd got the timetable wrong.

We'd dreamt of last things first, getting behind ourselves, like an urge,
          or a fault.
But there was plenty more, and we still had the air around our skin.

Weed Grounds

The way grounds become tired
of being told or dreamt

and weeds, from the work
of growing unattended, unregarded

they're ordinary, half-wild
and won't be stopped easily

by the great mutants
pests of language

attached and rootless in
the same unwelcome

beyond mirrors or concepts
meeting places

flowering and simply kidding
about being flowers

being sneaky and queer within
and beyond spaces

a bit part, a wall, a crack
broken field, a darkness

paths not quite flagrant
defiant and silly

a bitterness in fresh forms
taking and straying

Brushing Yonder

If you go north, it will get worse.
Valleys won't aid you.
The sun always goes down.
If you go west, you'll stumble.
All that reticence is fooling your shoes.
The moon hides in trenches.
If you go south, you'll drown, eventually.
You'll swell, you'll swivel, then flail
and capsize. It's always stormy.
If you go east, you'll survive.
But scarcely. There's no food.
The greens are dying, substances
rise and cover up the sky.

What if you stay here?
The hedge is full, the air blooms.
We're shot with care and perfume
of bare living, as roses rustle
parrots mass in yonder.
I could take your arm, nothing
banishes sorrow but that's no matter.
How root lives with skin
is the argument. There's always more
where apricots fall and lemons are flush
when you can almost believe, though
that's not enough.

It's what is more certain like a sun
like a phase, like a trice, a sudden brush
of direction. To dream of escape is
to form up the real and open your eyes
as if it was — again — morning.

Wind Shadow

Terra incognita transfers across a plain,
a wing blends the graces, tarmacs, macadam,
concrete being so concrete, the tar sick travel.
And hills make effort, rock, shrug, years of it,
as now we turn between cities.

Traction in flood water, blue slate,
red hollow, millennia forms feral, forms survival,
trail of goats, their black edges, hesitation
on the road, emu scrabble, kangaroo switch to flight,
twenty-one birds of prey, without prey,
dwelling along bright white civilised lines,
carrion mess and milky way, brutal shoulder,
bloody, in wind, in shadow, a kind of thinking, all there,
no matter what you dream, how uncomfortable,
this is where it happens, where it passes,
a creek bed, thunder clap.

'Return to find a river', to be faceless, this once,
off the grid, no identity, no thought but in itself,
going out of no paradise, 'where does memory live?'

To hear crows, thoughts pass, 'you blew it', the pace,
hurry days, in skirl, in concentration, 'return to
the living body', let the nothingness enter,
keep swinging in a body, your own laboratory,
work, push, and don't push, off centre, centre.

Smell grass, cow pats, new asphalt, let's be doing.

More Than Molecules

... non si densior aridis aristis
sit nostrae seges osculationis
    Catullus, #48

There are so many numbers
even in this field
the rocks, the grains, the grit.

Even if I counted the air
in all its nonchalant molecules
or the ways everything
grows after it dies, the grass
waving at us, if I could count
each shiver it makes
I'd still wish to touch you
ten thousand more times
kiss the time that's left
the time that leaves the grains
as we sit down, out in the field
which is dying, the great silos
which are dying, the trucks
the lands, the malls, the litter
the nuclear waste, all those
molecules too, everywhere.

To grow is to be deflowered
where we are is gone is never
enough to be touched.

Everything is Beautiful, Finally

Everything's burned   You thought it was entirely secular
Or a belief in the healing properties   of wounds or music
But now they've stolen our teeth
It's harder eating stones   until you learn drugs are dust
Strike each rock in time   until you shift it
As if there was more space   in the continuum

The weather is our fiction   And now here's the revenge
Slain minutes making rubbish   of flags and armbands
Pissing on excuses   commandments and jokes

It's getting worse   because it's getting worse   becomes our lie
Here's to the seething future   It's no longer obtuse or ambient
In the silent howl   material spell breaks
Or it's just fucking loud

Who says we will never part
We are together   Our waxworks are dying
Pooling, drying   in lumps like the fat we are
We're in the front row   We are the performance
We are testifying   We are terrifying   But no longer awesome
No longer transfiguring

Days are mangled   Sky's wrenched   The curtains are red
We put on the wedding dress   and we're becoming
The place of vows and sorrow   divorce and sundering
The shredding of ties and veils   suits, leaves, vibrations, temples
Choirs of formulas   The end of the affair   The last sail
The last monster   The beautiful drowning

Mighty Tree

I know what I dream.
It's impossible.
There are no ghosts.
They follow me.
The bus stop isn't a dream.
It's a mighty tree.
There is no camp fire here.
The dust is burning.
And all the exhaust.
The tickets are burning.
To dance with a ghost is real.
They catch on the occult lint of night time.
At the bus stop other things grow.
I'd rather walk back to night.
Its red and yellow planets.
Its luminous dome.
The day is more tenebrous than a dream.
Oh mighty tree fall on me.
Make me a legend or a nest.
The magpies can pluck my dream.
The ghosts can have the rest.

In This Wake

The shadow language
is falling, like trees
and broken rain

it's real now
like any other real
the inescapable

carbon monoxide you can
start to smell
in every face
the north face, the south

in every instrument
you touch
your lips to
for all the little disasters

playing along
the road that does not go
ever on, the mountain
you can't climb
out of respect, or absence

when even the dark is
stripped of its powers

The Woodland Chapel

Maybe death smells like pine needles and tar
to the living, maybe only roofs pray
and eventually everything falls
you go out in a long boat, burning

being alive is a representation of living
you can taste everything in your last meal
nothing is next, you can't see it
maybe you remember it like clouds

but all these vapours will be unmade
like the universe, this one or any other one

the utilitarian rows are no more eternal
or more useful than porticos, or burnt viscera
names, dates, and signs

so the golden angel dances at the chapel entrance
like any plastic angel, the wood-worn columns
rot near the stone paving

if you could cross the water forever you would
but the water is rising here
and dying there, it all goes in a wave
a breeze in time, a time like now

you go out in a long moment, burning

Skogskyrkogården

When The Green Starts

You dangle in sweet wreckage
escaping the doubt of the world
a small stone at the heart of the matter
or a shadowy self in dusty clothes
such a one who praises
a god of inversions.

Or you wander about purified
despite carbon, to breathe among
flowers bearing colour into the place
where dailiness stretches, grain by grain
or where it parallels your unstable night's
sudden chrome intersect, of silence
when the green starts
being brave, atomic

everything which is sung.

The Storm

The storm catches on the door.
It's a good sign, a surge that's more than breathing,
that blows away dirt from reliquaries,
and directions from their careful signs.
It's near speech and near trembling,
sky-bringer fate crowning from its centre,
if there was a centre rather than millennia
of waves, segmentation, volcanic chemistry.
And all this chlorophyll blowing around,
that does not understand solitude
but certainly vortex and rage,
the made and unmade clouds, constant phantoms
and caprices, the moving walls.
There is no void.   There is future,
no matter which way breaks,
the branch we find fallen on the new plants.
It's not a lucky escape from death, rust, abrasion, or bad thoughts
as I revise the possibilities within milliseconds.
A second doesn't describe any thought.
A thought doesn't show how I might want to run.
Time has nothing to do with what I hope to find
trembling in a gauge or written on a screen.
What passes is passing, and will pass.
If anything is eternal it is the motion,
as I step out to sweep what has gone and come.
The leaves make a noise almost as if
I was waiting for someone.

Where Wind Falls

If you surrender details
they gather 'a portion of the beauty'
in blue suburban clay.

In a clouded space
there's room to step shadows
where wind falls under the sun.

Ways you still
hear the grass
strata, fine planes, slips of craft.

But light leans in from the left
expecting more than
another opinion.

What do you need to know, to walk
land along the lines of its wounds.
Nothing is beyond question.

Disrepair

And what are they doing across the water?
Our boats are leaking this year, high on blocks,
ready, always ready for caulking, the repair
we've no time to give. And we listen for more
than half-silent scrapings of midnight
over the dunes, further than tides
recorded in old yellow quarto books.

There's been a rushing from over the water,
an impatience between wind and land,
against the years we've spent looking up
from our lines and tangled nets. We let
our hands alone find a way out of the maze
of knots we figure are enough for the catch.

We look for what they're doing over the water,
waiting for it to save us. Our boats are useless,
drawn up on the beach, spectators with our days
we work round. A stiff salt-sodden rope binds dawn
and the collapse at twilight. We prefer the constant
but casual wonder we float across the water.

Today we see the wind driving an old sloop
close into the shallows of the eastern cove.
The crew is small and they're tilted over the sides,
scanning the shore, as if calling for aid and repair.

Where the Sea Burns

... et lux perpetua luceat eis ...

No-one dies of the cold here, they say,
and talk instead of fire and smoke,
the dragon summer that consumed
matchbox houses of the abandoned village
which flourished once to the north.

Until fish began to die, they say,
all these strange twisted silver tongues
crying, crawling through the shallows,
flapping and gasping at last on grey sand.

And you could smell it for miles, some said.
A few survived, dragging slowly for days,
then disappeared into pools and lagoons where
there are silver lights over water at sunset.

But this is impossible, of course, nothing
lasts, nothing hopes under this heat and
nothing ever dies of the cold, they say,
not in the places, here and beyond, past
the cliffs to the north where the sea burns.

When Planets Softly Collide

This is not a poem about dust,
there have been too many of those,
but may be about wind, who knows,
the remaking of deserts, endlessly,
when sand becomes a definition
of scale or boundaries or change,
like weather squeezing out lines of heat
that drives from solid midnight freeze
up into the sweat pressure of midday.
These conditions are inescapable, no relief,
still there are flowers, stubborn and pink.

Yesterday, strangely, began with showers,
laying the heat demons down and out
for a moment and the air, wet
with the ghost of something old.
Whispers like clouds of aimless particles
which one day could form something solid,
whispers and the slight reverberation
of planets softly colliding,
showering each other with dust,
which they have been trying to avoid,
hoping for a poem about something greener.

As if rock didn't survive,
and dust didn't dance on air.

Poem Diesel Butterfly

The Wanderer Butterfly drifts
lands just beyond me
then rises
turns so
swift

Poetry actually does things
turns things
through the head ear page

    'Try that again'
syllable by
sound by sound
learning to count, magically

Language is a replica
like a market
Choose your words
    or does the poem choose you

Diesel infiltrates from the street
the noise of grading
a footpath

Clearing my throat means
something, clusters
of phrases
echo, guttural or charm

re -
    present
        even when sad
or distracted

The Wanderer appears again
taking no note of me
I think three syllables
but it's already gone
before I smile

I taste the bitter gas
New gutters must be laid
for important works

I hope we can still breathe

Winged

it is the centre of a word
that is unimaginable, almost
as it flutters out with the birds
indifferent over the lake

as closed in the eye
or as far as the mountain
brittle as a principle or a crust
in the hand

it is raised up but not grasping
the sides of the hours
it is suspended, it is surface
as though carried by water

or wind moves the parts of language
less calculable than the tides
not boxed or protected
once they leave the soft throat

the twist of autumn trees
lets down the light, trust
in the chill, naked and right
that winter will always be spoken

if it is tender as thinking inside today
and surrounding form — *pipipi*
little curlew will sing elsewhere than memory
raising sky with soundings/silences

but it is a kind of peace time
and also a form of force that emerges

such as words that rhyme
or shuffle softly near the tree

a head operates in its clay
and thinks about the wings
it cannot elevate to understanding
here against the fickle light

to be based on what is left
as though still unwritten
a statement that suddenly swerves
and disappears

it has moved beyond confidence
and shed that blunt examination
even though birds pick over the ground
that is written

Waking Alone By the Radio

I am recovering from too much
drinking or dreaming.
You're phoning from up-country
with woes of a drowned camera
(corrosion, insurance and bruises).
Yet you can visit frozen cobwebs
around the verandah.

Morning radio trickles in its woes and strangers
a little piece of sky burnt bright
as it fell over Sydney this morning.
Listen to the astronomers explain!
Then there's the world
all the contusions we know and don't know
(my knee or my dream is stiff where it clipped the floor).

You tell me that down by the creek
there were twelve baby platypus, with bright eyes.
They are curious, you say
and no bigger than your hand.

While All This is Going On

Rain comes at last over the quarry sides on a day grey as sandstone.
I reach across the skin of the house but can't find myself within.
The gate still sticks although the maple tree has healed itself.
Drugs pass across the road hand to hand. Somehow we all began
to sound like the shadow. Rage pelts trees all along the valley. The
sky isn't finished with us, not till the curfew. We realise there are
words inside words.

Windows blink, murmuring diamonds, and cast-off sounds twist
dreams.

You say: 'There are languages I regret not knowing'. Everyone
is working to the measure. How large it has become. We knew it
was all over after the cops had gone. Each second has a guard.
Unseen presences kick leaves and lever windows. We painted our
bars dark green where letters were torn. It isn't the time to hate.
We accept night and its measure where corners bend and rooms
rise up holy and self-contained. We don't always understand the
noise, but take comfort in storm light. Air is transparent beyond
the hill, towards the bay. We are washed in salt and amusements,
immersed then drawn more slowly as our selves. Drops of
mosquito poetry climb my arms but my blood is elsewhere, serum
with the droning and diving world. All I want is a breeze at an
open window, to watch a raven lift, black, shadowed, astonished.

Sea and Star

I walk from one memory
held on my arm
to another told
like the sea.

I walk from one time
that counts itself
to another unwound
and turned.

How far back?
Past the reef
past the mound
where the rocks once grew.
Memory — the faint star.

from Limits We've Shouldered

Futures and Stardust

A mesh that is not so seamless.

Those little dings and impossibilities.

Glow out of the big sky.

Innocence is a universe — but not sanctuary.

If friends crash and faces are hollow.

If the thrilling emptiness is just a biology.

Kiss the children between the lies.

Stoke our whitewashed outlines.

Touching the walls, what is common.

Your cool skin maybe but breathing.

Beyond the stages of importance.

Burrow into the sweeter afternoon.

Perhaps the stardust song settles it.

It must get easier out in black.

What flowers, we don't know yet.

What remains, what you touch.

It is like a photograph, you step into it.

It is like space.

Futurism at Night

I stayed up all night under the world's dangling lamp and the shadow did not eclipse it. I toed the Bokharan prayer mats and struggled with words along the green stripe of the sofa. Of this, I am still accused, as though I had thrown the first fruits at angels and glued the hems of avatars to chair legs. I acknowledge the night is open to speed and the push beyond pages, an overthrow of slow velvet edges, but this is not war, the generals merely look sick in the blue light and a tank twists in the ditch outside. Across the fat cushions, along the hallway and around the cornices are my placements but when I hit the road you will really see that lamp swing, zooming beyond sense everyday. It's got past the eternal now, each sentence talks from another in the house and paragraphs tangle. You cannot unwire them as they conflict and kiss, spreading tissue into tissue. Accuse me of some moist blaspheming or of dropping articles as though I cannot be definite as an army. Little lamp no slower than searchlights or blazes. Sentence searching for another — zoom, zam, *zaum* — as it grows.

Leaving it to the Sky

I don't belong to generation green. I look out onto slate tiles. Finally, there's rain on iron; but piss-weak. My phone falls so easily off the table. I don't believe in fake tans, but I could. All around are little dogs. Hail, queens of suburbia! Every so often, it's the age of beige. Perhaps you could win a sedan, be in business, not be a wanker. I remember Friday's laughter down by the river. But the swans aren't wild, just nasty. I'll never be a unit-shifter. I can't explain why.

Wastage, control, a single low call rate. You can't be serious! If you redefine The Problem That Has No Name, would we be here at all? It's more than the mind-body poser. What will make us think? No-one gets along in the news. I've been on most of the rides. Am I my own provocateur? I look upon the Westpac building and trace its sky tentacles. This is an historic street with its geraniums, bottlebrush and roses. And it's a windy Sunday; hear the bells of St Somewhere in the city of quietude.

I'm thinking about my father's ukulele, lost things, the ink patterns between east and west. Transcontinental! Whichever way the weather moves, it's depending on blue. I've never been relaxed and comfortable. Why does he yell like that? All the space is above; over green iron, city plans, the curve of sky is lost. I'm relying on radio, voices, distance. All around, there's a smell of toast and tomatoes. I'm having a yak with a piece of paper.

So, am I famous for not being famous? Do I lack an over-arching narrative? Leave that to the sky, give me Iced Vo-vos, cups of strong tea, and a work ethic. The smell of coffee says something. About me? Flesh imagines me back east, the desert imagines nothing I imagine.

A machine begins
noisy like all the machines
of our lives.
The rain that never was
has stopped.

Screens, Jets, Heaven

Lightning above the bay.
Sky night shimmers.
We almost scent rain.
Jet engines shudder on curfew
then cease.
Rain doesn't come.
The hills shape the clouds.
Blind stars — always.
By midnight they are covered
with the noise of our life.

We know heaven's vacant.
But on screen we're beautiful
in the pulse of cables,
our light in a flickering frame,
the neon of a dirty world.

The midnight special
screens old rock and roll
a purity in black and white moves.
So we find solace
when we peel back the covers.
We sing raw
but still beautiful
skimming light from a song
wrecking harmony, sublime
and nonchalant.

Dawn sneaks us in, awakened.
A new wind is in from the south.
Out there the sea,
the new day's jets.

The New Aesthetic

You've heard this story before —
becoming unravelled in Europe
or assaulted in some roadhouse
but bold as nipples and booted.
Recovering with bourbon and red wine
in a soft room with a German
dissolving somehow at right angles
and falling off the frequent flyers list.

Or being born in a blood thrust
from shadows into that crazy moment
as a rocket strafes the moon
ghosting your hour of the dog.
It's a kind of domino effect
taken out of context
while babies murmur in the lagoon —
another supple peepshow.

The Tender Stone

The pen so cold
snow edging the city
wind tests the monuments
their verdigris work of the soul.

There'll always be dancing
at the bar americain
though the tongue freezes
without speech.

All along the boulevard
people press their lives
into the sounds
in their heads.

There's something tender in stone
cold frees it
the living stand with flowers
feel the coming sleet.

Water is more than rain
There's no sleep beyond the night
and now is always interruption
sweeping away leaves.

I cover my head
where the cold falls.

Cimetière Montparnasse

Laundromat Near the Corner of Passage Alexandrine

Here's to centuries of laundromats
and cigarettes, boundless fluorescence
and the coin slot, time and heat, clean towels
for all, the warmth of euros as they descend,
detergent named for animals or angels.
It's minus one, it's six o'clock and the moon
is already busy. Here, everything folds
after it spins, according to the politesse
of strangers. The room is full of greetings,
water runs all over our clothes as though
it had always meant to do so.

It's time to turn and let the colours be
they will never stay sharp, not even
in moonlight, as fibres fray and fall till
they can no further. This is no longer
important, although we have nowhere
to go that's changed from this morning.
It was sunnier then, of course, but
what metamorphosis could we accept
so late in the moment when we have
nowhere else to go in our centuries,
our waters, or our winters that are shiny
in each uncertainty.

Seeds

It's a concept that revolves
around flowers
that represents both the time
being and the time lost.

The future is all
that's present
in these other times
bloom and dust

a residue of carnation
rose and chlorophyll,
old worlds
remaking old worlds

here and now.

Listen, vases topple
and roots
become bone in the earth
that recycles us.

We are weeds and trees.
My petals fall
like seeds.

Cimetière Montparnasse

A Piece of Everything

I walk over the discarded skin
of the world

the tree keeps falling while
it stands

I walk on myself and millions

sunlight seems to waver

everyday I hold a piece
of everything

insect dust, guano, a feather

my own ashes
awaiting

Wild Curious Air

I walk through the curious air.
   I feel earth thrust and scrape.

Each plant breath
   unveils me as shadow guest
in the wild space of afternoon.

All shadows have their own colours.
The next day and the next
   are unfinished.

Let's stride out anyway
   fresh-ancient   mortal

4.

the way the air touches you, if it's free or heavy

The Thought of an Autobiographical Poem Troubles & Eludes Me

So I've been leaning against
the names of things
not just walls but the very air
the rug, the pen
the silver garbage bin.

But all words are
autobiographies
used to tell
half sentences
a quarter turning moon.

Today is a sound.
I hear words that mean
landing jet or rustled plastic
a book that depends on mercy.
And the gas, breathing.

I Am, I

I am, I am a little, I am
a parcel, I am yet
I dreamed this mortal
I grew up bent

I had a picture, I hear a river
I like a ship in storms, I put
your leaves aside, I remember
the clumsy

I saw the spiders, I struck
the board, I that have been
I, too, I wrote in
the dark

Antipodean Geography

Continents on the wall
shift slowly through a tide of weather.
Cupboards open and laugh.

Great seabirds on the ceiling find their own
longitude, and carry
what's forgotten to lagoons beyond the door.

There you could swim
safely, and tides are kinder than the wind.
It's the Antipodes!

Lost and found again, so you may
find her now and then,
beyond glass and wood, fibres of rooms.

Proud on the sill, a bird.
Its yellow eye looks past the sofa to valleys
that sing. And vases of mountains

burn darkly.

Bohemian Rhapsody

You drove all night
following shooting stars

Take it easy, desperado
we're all wanderers again

Listen
there is sound out here

Let's spend the times
and the changes

You're a wave
so oscillate wildly

No dictation tests
in the moon glow

Once the oxygen's gone
the fun begins

In the cosmic ah-um
you're laughing

Remains remain after first thought
fades in millennia fever

Here are our thousand dances
so, don't be afraid

Viva, viva the real
and the nights together

Round Midnight

You're home again and things click, getting ready
along with the fridge door popping. Flames, fruit, tea leaves
and the sound of news pages turning side by side.

No longer is the kitchen a mournful song overlooking
the long backyard. Water hustles preparation and wine
is a song that doesn't need sipping, whether it's red
or just a riff we remember together. I'm OK — you know
I'll always say this — but each minute makes its point
and an hour belongs to time again. Not that sitting down with
the expanse around midnight is a pointless activity.

I've done those stretches and come up bold enough.
But now this window is ready to include our shoulders,
my timing, your newest narrative. No-one else
needs to know in what other ways we can excel.

Heat in a Room

January soaks the hill with white sky
grass writes into blood and a river of heat sings

Music loads the morning with legends
an afterimage of crowds reaching into a room

Small dried packages of territory remain unturned
there is whispering outside under the redemption of intervals

Just as silence deciphers light
exchange rates cycle gently through conversations

And days draft me, breathing extinction
my skin a chassis of orange

As for the car, it shimmers into the raging sunset
then sort of erupts

(a kind of persistent hope that nobody gets caught)

The night's hangers are loose in the closet
sleep is a projection, part of the weightlessness

It is impending — a delicate sense of the flange
it seems as though the room is small.

Grass

Empty girl I was, so far inside, grass didn't know me

It was something unbending, only light seemed to touch

But so long as I could smell the sea, so long as salt

I had extrications, music, that fire, phase and beat

And all around the world went off, banners and avenues, cruelties

Now it's come one, come all, a kind of sassy hoedown

The grass is going, it cracks and withers sadly, almost infinitely

But I'm becoming younger as my dead drugs strangle each-to-each

I go out with skin mixes, cantos and some fear rocking

I stand or fall but now I can feel that region's joy, the bones

To Sleep Inside Rain

A hazy field
rain cast plummeting
plunge of stone hallways
to our bed's name
something
like daisies in place
if not sweet
there is daring.

Rolling into excess
thighs out of tight labels
above nerves
worm among
creases, access
rolling out alive
bloomed sunflowers
crossing light with surface
inside rain.

The effulgence: screen, expanse
the slightest intent
violet flower promises
beneath dark.

That death as good as earth
a little, like sun oblivion

then lie still.

The Dress Sonnet

I have taken off my little dress, there's no scope
for me within it, there are things
that fall down the body, like breath and the texture
of the flap. This is a button I can't do.
I don't want to argue on the easy side. 'Don't expect
an audience or a reveal.' O, the little dress
shimmers in the near breeze as I'm falling down
my body and, at last with my ear to the ground

it's too late in the season to please as wind removes
my feathers and shaves my bones with that first whip
of change, and each winter, if it comes along, do I
need its great coat, will I have done with cumbered sleeves?
Sometimes I could do with the humour of a petticoat.
O, let me part the clouds, let me in.

I Welcome Night's Ruins

Night is the oldest of ruins I know.
But everything seems exact. I tell myself
there's no sin in looking backwards
if that's where the monsters went.

I listen for damage as something
crashes, is it a book or simply shapes
of things, a kind of blue after
midnight? A hundred translations.

The house itself isn't done or alone.
Where are all these extras? I remember
curtains but that doesn't help.
What sort of ghost do I prefer?

When I was born, night thought
about me, then later found me.
I'm still singing that song in the
thickets of its generous haunting.

'It doesn't hurt to fall off the moon'

When night is naked,
it risks as much as us.
My mind spills like water.
You launch yourself into it.

Even while we're kidding around,
I unpack all your knots.
'What if we try this?'
What if we change each other.

Knots are possibilities. I weave them
out of themselves, tenderly,
curiously, like a charm,
or a plot difficult to relate.

How do women chase each other?
Teamwork, I guess, as we put each other
on, exchanging clothes neither of us
need. It becomes beautiful slapstick.

We fall into and out of each other
as reflections across a lake.
The night isn't tame or duplicitous.
We stroke and steer by the hours.

Your breath is my river.
I row with you into morning.

The Night Before Your Return

The night is kind tonight,
the sky is purple,
clouds are orange,
and planes fly away
to the south.
I need no fan, a cricket sings.

And you are under heat in Brisbane.

The kids next door do not sing,
one phone over the road softly rings,
and I have drunk pale green tea
from an old cup.
I have not done
what I ought to have done.
The window is open
as the mind at midnight,
cars fade away,
carriages rattle through timetables.

You are asleep and out of range.

Spiders work, their lines
arrange like poetry,
another train embraces
the lone traveller,
and there are always the dogs.
I am clean, naked and cool.

You are covered in distance
that you unwrap tomorrow,
driving down

over rivers, across valleys,
through hot towns, dry acres,
into the wet south of my dreams.

Consummations

the spinning world
     the guttural dark
sounds the skin   & leaves you
     a book of consummations
fresh as rot & queer within

*

in the torn fabric
     the ancient salvage
it's all moving
     clues   charms   throngs
the dearest ground

*

exhale
     between breath bones
no moment more free
     horizon   potent
enough to be touched

As Long as You Need / Fragments

As if a cute-voiced girl
in the slack limbs of eros
sweet and bitter
I still shudder.

They say don't disturb
all that washed-up trash.
Now the sea's sour as death
do I still miss all that ... darlin'?

Remember our burlesque hearts
and heads relaxing on sweaty breasts
in Sydney's sun ecstasy
in its dusk-pink twinky hours.

Remember making our way
among shadowy electro-shapes
no party too hot ... no dance
where we were absent.

In an old century! Of course
we did such flash young things
such wasted perfect time
such girls all those nights up long.

My mind now cracks up
as the world's fucked.
Pink and purple blossoms
rot on the footpath.

If this is my shame or pride
I must speak for what

the future will recall … even
my own disturbing junk heap.

Still … to the ends of the earth
Desires! all of them older
all of them younger all now
still lifting above the roof.

… in fabulous style … just like
honey … for as long
as you need … with these
two arms …

What the Glass Holds

The shape of the glass
is not the same
as what the glass holds.

The shape of the water
is infinite pleasure
inside bodies
and around them.

The shape of the glass
reminds me of the night
you first arrived.

The shape curves
in my hand.

The glass is the shape
of morning and night.

The glass reflects
the green and yellow light
from the garden
and the water there
in the air and
the ground.

The water tastes of all
and nothing, of its
internal bonds, of
where it's been.

The shape of the glass
may one day break.
Water may break.
We will too, into our
water, air and ground.
Today is every day
until then.

I drink to all that.
To what the glass holds.
And what it doesn't.

Oh Venus, That Zenith

In the morning media rustle
we look for our vertebrae
    our balance, anything sensible
        shoes or daycream
encase our nipples although
    we fancy being free
as the train gushes and swallows
    tickets and selfies, hi-vis
        and daydream

Then the city's coarse daylight
opens its cracks
    the paving jerk, escalator drag
        a last gulp
so our mouths might swell
    with sexual tannins
        a café's smoke tongue
before swipe and thrust

Goodbye cruel air, you weepy green trees
    crushed yellow light
The lift slackens to the tenth floor
We remember nothing now
apart from the gash in night
    good ol' dog Sleep
running about under red moon
    and white cliffs and how
        we fall there, and there

Oh Venus I don't forget you
    in the spread
of tinted morning, the grids

I've wandered far in circles
   around your heights
without shoes or sensibilities
     I don't forget you
and how I've climbed
into another balance, cusp
   flexure, fold
another arc and then
another

Happy Families

You've come from afar
a little beam
into a small warm room.

People are waiting.
You don't know how to say it
the thing they wait for.

You don't even know
you're supposed to say something.
It's not even a decision.

Your own genius spooks
it runs to the cupboard
and breaks all the plates.

You stare at the old yard
and ignore all that poetry
in the kitchen.

Even the fridge sings.

Fractures

I have eaten words
all night for years
splitting bone and lies
enamel dreams.

My bruised canine
is stitched behind my face.
Count them! Three knots
above the root
of ink and troubled pitch.

Tremble, mouth-bitten desire
pulped fantastic
on night's ink
where fancy creeps.

My wolf vision
now spit and listerine
blood burning
codeine prey in throat.

I Must Be With You in the Cold Time

I've lost my sensitivity, you say.
That was always possible
along with a fear of breathing.
As though this was intentional.

I watch as bucket loads drop
then slowly decrease.
I go into work tasting of externals.
I've wished an end, nevertheless.

Elasticity is a way round ascension
after a time of emptiness.
A world is stored in whole numbers.
I agree, my absentee moves too hard.

Fear at night blanks inner recovery.
Each word is sent without meaning.
Conceit's attributes rupture in body.
Psycho-technology witnesses my sketchiness.

I'm hungry with these skinny solutions.
My sweat thickens the walls of an hour.
Even the packages are vanilla wrapped.
I wish for response rather than a flip-phone.

'La Vida Loca'

'I wanted to get lost in the city'
someone came up the drive

'I guess you two know each other'
it'll take time

we'll make a long story even longer
going to sleep stretches the night

enjoying the acrobat music
needing to move, 'to do nothing'

it was a lot of work to finish high school
one day I picked up the phone

I flew to Mexico City
next Friday I debuted in this show

in the first six months I realised
'talk to me yeah baby'

after the show I hopped a plane, went to Italy
'like, every woman in history'

living la vida loca
imagine the press release

'I stopped for a second'
I'll die and think about those days

I need to play with my dogs
I look in the mirror in a Japanese hotel

what became of the weeklong party?

These Things (braided)

How   the city Was grey though   it was Summer   and
everyone   was thinking   Christmas   holidays
A siren runs past   the night And   it almost
enters me Like   an alarm already   my body
Is   full   of alarm Can   I hold   your hand It   will
make me   less alarmed It   will make Me more
for   panic The   siren   is   no excuse What   if
someone is dying   they   treat You   tenderly but
firmly In   an   ambulance you feel   so alive Like   a
body feels as   avenues Pass   you or you   pass them I   am
easy   to see Even   in cool   wintry Dark
Perhaps   I could be   a beach Or   part of   an ocean
Once   that would   have seemed Swell   but now it's
dirty   as   everything Perhaps   yes   that siren Perhaps   no

Or   a   meteor's tail That   streaked over   the
city Last   Tuesday   like an alarm   I didn't   see it Somebody
did   I   usually miss These   things I daydream   at
coagulating Full   of whistles   Indirection bad chapters
Misquotes   infusions A   plastic   hum I'm   not prepared
passing as a Human As   a woman As   a   life form With   as
much skin They   attach a monitor I   Remember   that
night And   read old stories of   a coach That   arrives
for me   at last It   makes Little sound   the horses
However   are anxious   they know It's   time for
me   to go They   know it's time for   us all
They   know how   to see What   should be
alarmed Someone   will   see us   It   is Difficult to bear
the thought Of   being in the shape   I'm in

Cursing Girl Gust

o what! spare us   heroes & *heofen*
though I look like   the almost-you
there is other craft   rare & raw
in my wit's hoard

I have no show-brag   trick kiss
my uncomely   dross-dress
plain-face hide   & hunch-mind
my down-dark   leant in cunning

fuck you fey-fickle foe   pest-face
you'll not play in the   cut of me
don't sweet-wif me   wanker
you sack-head creep   between walls

what am I   your nemesis
yr woe & yr drag   yr big fall
so you shall   to yr dust-world
no-heaven   I'll do the cut of you

I was tough-wrought   ain't yet wreck
but so long you   so heck you
I'm cloud-friend   & storm-born
the not-this not-that   you bet yr other

I Am Brushing Myself

shed skin like roses   share genders like perfume
shed skin like the dying tree   the day like its roses

smell lemon-scented gum   smell lemon   lick
genders like the yellow lemons in my hand   the rose

petals   white pink and yellow   on my shoulders
brown bark skin   the day shares its genders

all over my hands   stickiness   a prickle
the bug's orange life   the stamen's saffron life

the rich black loam   the shaky leaf   green
milk cut   the dead gum bleeding away   sap life

as agendas blow away at my feet   the changing air
as the kids play   somewhere over   the dog next door

whimpers and air floats the day   I am brushing
myself within in it   this petal   this dust that enters me

as I am less or more than   the human as if roses or lemon
-scented   or rainbow-winged   or diesel-fleshed   or

air trails of smoke   or neighbourhood cheers   or
the lost beetle among   whatever   leaves are left

whatever   grit is needed   in roots

The Un-Marvelling

How strange last night, I beheld your face, electric
with thought along with my unrest, alight and hollow
when the night trees shivered and the block
we walked seemed more cluttered than the road
we used to walk, where every little plot
and fence was tended, maybe we were too narrow
maybe we lost our hunger then to care or look
to stare at stars, to forget the way we marvelled
how their brightness could also seem soft
and how the moonlight would seem to strain
through the canopy no matter how intense or thick
how this strange loveliness may never come again
how I wanted something — something I never quite got

An End of Flight

The bird trembles before it dies.
Why are you holding it?
You're in a strange land. The trees are dark.
The bird's colours are like your land
where you're also a stranger behind
the terrible glass walls that seem free and bright.

Darkness and light aren't simply arguments
about doors, shelter, daubs of thought.
You don't know what this small parrot
heard, what it saw. Home or flight
aren't simply discourse or headlines.

Glass is composed by heat and sand
soda ash and limestone.
It's only so far flexible. It's cold. There's a mark
where the bird struck. It dies
and your hands tremble with stupidity.

You will go back out into a stranger's yard
to bury it. Their yard?
A borrowing. All concepts are theft.
Even the earth is no longer primaeval
but roots tremble as the wind moves branches.

Borders are always moving.
Where will you dig?
Soon someone will come in.

There's nothing tidy in any of this.
Any moment it will rain.

Mouth Form Flower

Let fault flaw
Let the fence fall
Let's flabbergast the goal with tongues
Let debacle warp in dawn
Let beginning bury end
Let a hundred pods blush

Let the mouth form flower
Let flesh flash
Let's lick plethora
Let erosion jabber in the gown
Let's find fit and make do
Let's sieve without shock

Let debris fill rust
Let myriad dapple and draw
Let's spurn our quote marks
Let's trick death perception
Let limit out
Let not mere quintessentials

Let wreckless wreck more
Let cloth drop
Let's lay waste the hours

Let's not say

Let a thousand errors bloom

Touches / Touches Us

Everything Touches

If there is light   there
must be dark   if in   the dark
   you wait a   while   un
til   a different   moon re
turns there's no   proper   distance

After Mark Rothko, '#20'

RootSky

darklight   darkdog sleeps
a tree grows   in the heart we're
   cloudmud children   you
give me plant   fire   I'm a cre
vasse   blood   flowers milkdrop   earth

*After Frida Kahlo, 'The love embrace of the universe
the Earth (Mexico), Diego, me and Señor Xólotl*

Your Eyelashes Like Grass

   our pores   bloom   like roses
I sweep   dust out the   door its
   threads   blushes   tiny
flora   an interstellar
wind   carves nebulas   like grass

After Jackson Pollock, 'Autumn Rhythm'

'Everything should be blue. But is it?'

what fell   from weather
o fabulous   mutinous
     machine   bending blue
waves   islands   flaking off sky
stacks   skerries   makeshifts   singing

After Wilhelmina Barns-Graham,
'Variations on a Theme —Splintered Ice No. 2'

To go home   to the old home

to make   of spittle
and milk   to spill   as all   pig
ment   blood to   the fire
utterance   'oh'   uterus
nipple   tree   dirt   leaf   black moon

After Paul Klee, 'Wald-Hexen' (Forest Witches)

~~what doesn't~~ Touch us   ~~hovers all~~ The same

     waves   skulls   skin   seaweed
a flotilla   tangled lines
     even   the invis
ible has   sound   oars drag   storm
ferocious   hours   tide loves

After Cy Twombly, 'Lepanto Part III'

162

Let Loose Looks

A woman looks among
A tree looks like a woman looks
On a refuse looks with a salvage looks
After another looks along a shelf
Looks into a self looks
Between a path

Looks over an accident looks despite
A blood clot looks following an advance
Looks under a shoe
Looks minus a drink looks round
A dream looks on a handle
Looks past

A roundabout looks for a rescue
Looks without a ring
Looks opposite a conspiracy
Looks to a lamp looks since a wound looks
Amid two looks as what looks like looks

Self and branch and air and secret and a bloody mess
And beauty and what's left
To the children to the smell of sweat
Alongside the train with the fresh feet following a shot
And a muscle

Looks but a branch looks like a brand looks as a fire feels and looks
And the way through with the sign with the nothings among
The extras with variables with adoration with rain

Between latitudes via neverending with a basket
With furlongs to markets among songs

And diversions with the hammer
With the weeds along the flesh
And vectors despite the bandages

Through the prism with chains
And with rather than outworn
Or nonsense or vicious or drastic

A garden tastes like a woman looks as looks let loose looks
To tastes as selves
Paths refuse wounds
Rescues sweats sweet

The Dissolve

Have you admitted something is catching
on the gate?
Is it the way a wind blows
out of the mouth of spring
the crackle and crisp touching up
of a skinny evening?
How the flowers move above their shadows
black leaves, green hearts
lines of worms and bugs written on leaves.
But you cannot exhaust your head
or put it down
heavily.

Though the city makes you tender
at times it seems you were never
part of it — here.
Elsewhere nothing seems true
but loose as a whisper, part of the dissolve.
With a glance of the hand
you are heaping the forgotten
rather than attending to the laying down.
Currawongs from a day's mist blanket
remind you, echoed as a lone girl
while all this obstructed rippling
is slowed down to drift in the passing cold.

Tell me how it's undone —
moving between the birds, the cracking trees
over a fence as I taste wind furl
past ghost lips, the never blue light
my house, my intersection —
to arrange the chill then light up the knots

to experience the labour
that now unshapes me.

Figure

I'm sometimes very like me.
I can't get rid of the
poor little nonsense!

What can self do
with such visions?

Look at everything
with eyes
skirting the obscene.

Push on through
tearing the robe
exciting suspicions.

Always holding a little figure
something striking
very like me.

Afternoon Grey In

Afternoon grey in afternoon sounding
not like a sign but a soughing
which is white over the night shoulder
bent with market crash not soughing
not sighing and never sign anything
you download in the grey afternoon
but let it and let it out and letting go
something with beautiful grey sounding
more beautiful that is going beautiful
in the garden is sometimes red or
sometimes pink and fall leaves all petaline
where more rain predicts more rain and rain
that is lovely letting go of something
that clicks before a storm do not click
do not buy but let go before the night
storm over your shoulder beautiful and
waiting for the moon changes its large
light that is not and not grey nor slim
not an insert not alternative not faux simple
not resounding but the coming moon
that cycles with that enduring the wind
touches and it touches where you grey
impermanent sounding sigh in a lithe
shoulder before you go down into before
you petals leaves and leaves you

5.

it's a long time since I've come home this way

Into Our Thin Rivers

My father dies in the night
That afternoon he said to us 'get me out of here'
I know this is what the doctors have done
It's called pain killing
The next day we go to see him
His face is colder than I'd ever imagined

My mother dies at an hour I'm not told
It took less than a year
She floated on a general anaesthetic
up a river I'd never heard of
into a small room
where at the end she could say nothing

As a child I remember them covering my face
and the ticking machine that was also a river
a dark delta land full of birds
I remember its ether breath
I sometimes still smell it in my dreams
I wonder who decides to turn it off

Night Visitor

As if he means no harm, walking into the dream room, childhood. He seems to know it, stepping between single beds of memory, sure and faceless. I try to speak the question or unveil the name in his absent eyes but at my sound he vanishes, the stairs are silent, thin black air. One night he stood still under the skylight, huge as a door, but more often he's wandered the hallway or the foot of this wider bed. He's called by a tight band beating, irregular, across my ribs, hears my brain's low tide lapping the moon. A year ago, he was tall and thin, a sheaf of flowers clasped heavy below his head. He reached down but couldn't touch me. I lay there calling. For three days after he stalked the semi-circle, refusing to leave the night. All he wanted was a place for his flowers, a low place across my breath. Tonight, he's brought the past into my room, shuffled rhythms a heart like mine hurries onto the only future sure to pass. He's stepped between shadows, sure as solid, as winter dark. If he speaks, I'll vow to nothing, leaving the air open for retrieval, sirens and the blood orange dawn.

Big Flower

I haven't had that dream again
night visitor death and the big flower
I did not even die but rose
through the strata, plains of clouds
beams, quivers, satellites, walkers
to the place the moon might be
somewhere around earth but
just a slip eastward, northward
in the shaky sky beyond the sky
where the birds come from where
they all talked on the ground
before trees looked like trees
when I was young I dreamed of
tunnels, of walking passages
of hydrangeas to blue-green death
but I did not die I flew
I thought this proved something
or would make me content with
the way things were, wearisome
worthwhile or perhaps just wonky.

Death knows me, the moon knows
me, I see that smile on the birds
that know me in the tree
to the northeast, me, their bright
bodies the least of my preparations.

'I only wanted to see what the garden was like'

Whether slovenly or splendid
I'm leaning into
the darkness yet again

As if I was a disbanded girl
whose lucid life
was called inside

My smashed vision
misses everything
but the detours and shade

How should I make
myself different
With an identity pass
or redactions

I have boxes of medicine
for everything
flowers of sulphur and restoratives
amphetamine lip balm

I tremor before reality
I have no electronic desire

I spend an hour staring
at a verb
It stares back
It knows I'm fraudulent

I think about my dreams
of mutiny
and burn the poems

I have this old memory
of objects on a table
a blind mirror, a severe dark rose
a cruel figurine
Who will explain them to me

Or how to re-enter the world
in the morning
as a child in the garden
unreachable and endless

Possible Manners Of Revelation

I translate roses as multiples, a rose and a rose and a rose

I paint all my corners different colours

I welcome my own redundancies, and all that time to kill

I resurrect the dead for a second when I close my eyes

I slide that agnostic load from my shoulders in a flash of unearthing

I face east then west to respect my indirection

I swallow the moonlight and hope it may ward off the sincere and
embarrassing shadows I've shed

I return to multiples

I alphabetise my dreams hoping for order

I set fire to my opinions and wait for the truce

I find lost amulets in the gutter left by cyclists or the stars and
bless them again with unchained secrets

I strike light into the dark passage where the summer moths return

I forget my body is what I have with me until my fingers and
breath do their work

I tinker with the time it takes to remember

I remember everyone I forgot

I promise the invisible I will return one day

I lean against the transcendent, listening to the honeyeaters fight in
the camellias

I talk to absence like the one who has gone

I ask emptiness to fill me

I deface all my damage because the world won't forgive me

I recite a history of my own breath, which is the poem

Elegiac Continuum

As though I'd lived in some days that felt
right, but in others where I felt all the gas was gone,
our horoscopes crumpling like wacky movie sets
whose details were out-of-time in the bogus light.
As we passed the tremendous neon present
and its wanton sparkle, every toy
was us and smelled of pine air freshener.

I was writing again, to no-one, but diligently
painfully, then out of the blue, I demounted
from the truck into a baffling, besotted twilight.
It spoke as I used to speak, a voice, defiant as
the crushed but beating world. Perhaps
it was chance, a ghost, the machine of the heart
my bloody old nerve, still singing the continuum.

from My Fugitive Votive

Day is clouds and earth in our crisp, bitter bodies,
as kids toss balls into their game.   'Someday I'll fly away'.
I know my old theories are 'no longer useful'.
I'd rather it be granular, lapidary, a cut-up.   Full o'flack
I must be careful as I rise into the general rain. 'Listen,
can no method save it', history, time, the water table.
If save not these gutters, so I love them for their trash
as our umbrellas whisk the wicked lanes.

Thunderheads sometimes intrude, lower themselves, saying
'who can I run to, out into low sky?', someone twists a machine,
leaves wash under green sun and processes inside me
tremble and stutter. I want to picture this, as if capturing
souls departing on wax or an old glass plate   in a garden
asking for ascent like doves, all debatable, beautiful and bruised.

& the white flowers live inside themselves   still as water
its slow ripple climbs the hill.

Break On Through

I remember part of my bootleg
something boiling over
but someone still had
an eye on the game
the serene, small television
I was original mono
someone was singing
like milk happening
psychedelic ball pock bang
the dogs were touching
things with changelings
charged with damages emptying
the fire extinguisher
into the ash tray I'm taking
notes then must sing them
expedition to a place
where I can think
the end being the apex
hypnotic sound from
someone's hands on
the vox turned low I remember
being pulled down a road
I had to stop miming
my watch though
time keeps going
begins to end static
wires tubes and batteries
only present crackles
within the harmonium
and sublime's shaky hands
I was original bootleg
vox hypno and charge

A Fantasia of Oddments, Wagers and Zeroes

In the midst of afternoon   an unexpected hubbub above
parrots midair chasing a falcon   sun in my eyes I brush
light   the radiant-shaking leaves loosed from their crib
my first time free of blame for my ill-feeling   my dank
self-pity as a citizen of pain   sun's mocking me, its empire
large, ancient   while I cope with presence, motes, a fantasia
of being   even as small as the life forms on my skin greater
than earth's population   do they feel guilty like their host
or are they me   mostly empty, waiting for batteries, innards
sounding a sonorous plaint   I bless every idea, glance and jot
in my creases   as starlight feels its way, seems ever so keen
as I step forward slowly   shading my eyes from the luxury
the day's slough taste, plant oil, insect   joy of the meld
lifedeathlife nectar   planets as gods above it all, the nuzzle
of eternity terrors   while I'm heaving my ribs and oddments
looking for nightcusp   wineblood's less to blame, let it pour
with the backyard gladness, the universe honey   the quick
and freight of littlebig world, its evildoing   or pitiless raddle
of my circulation, CO_2 emissions, the west's bountiful sophistry
the wasteland of antibiotics, water features, and trolls
oh wait, honeyeaters hustle and drop   and I'm so ugh
wondering when all the oil will be gone   leaving vitriol
or a spangled release, an unguessed drug   or a wager
as if this is my portion I grab at the door   nothing x-ray
could determine   my mind's not a printout, it's a yammer
of lyric passionate as a forest   lost songs, the zeroes

from The Plover in the Poem and What Meaning Does Not Mean

17.

I am moving things around.

I am considering pencils.

I see thirteen ways I can pile up papers.

I realise where the mistakes will fit.

I get anxious about moving things around.

I wonder if at night things move around.

I can think of seventeen things to do with mistakes.

I understand anxiety is normal.

I hear the night — it's night already.

I don't know what to say about night.

Is my anxiety insanely adorable?

I get up and go home.

Difficult Poem

(yeah, like a

lucid tiff   fit of plum   dolt cuff

epic mould   cute plod   dulcet mop

coiffed lump   polemic fit   demotic puff

muffled tic   code flip   deficit flop

melodic if   cleft podium   iced muff

tumid elf   difficult mope   lucid top

Dreaming Homeward

Where shall there be an end of old and new
— Li He, 'On and on for ever', trs A. C. Graham

Here are ten thousand changes, shading
sky and earth, along the river's mask.

What arrivals does it know
when all journeys dream homeward?

Is there a raft that can carry me?

I drift. Does it matter if I fail
under cloud spell?

I scrape light to its bones
keep guessing, water's true colours.

— after 'Riverbend', Sidney Nolan

The Green Dress

The desert erases regard, wind plays on.
A mirror looks back to the future which has no face.

I'm a player for the war outside.
My name has killed me, vaterland, vaster land, no escape.

Do not forsake me!
I've become the most beautiful green dress.

Maybe you would not recognise me
when the Johnnies come marching home.

— after 'Snow White Joins Up', Klaus Friedeberger

A Taste For Hunger

I've put my hand out to the word.
It's been there for days. Hovering
between the newspaper and the television.

It's been crying. I can tell this pain. The pulling
apart. Pages in telephone books and directories,
their rough skins drag the air.

It's between the kitchen's song — making,
a smell of it. What's left in the corner,
wrapped in old newspaper — And

a song of living rooms, steady humming.
An excuse for silence these days.
And when the crying doesn't stop

the word becomes water bowl,
salty in making. This taste of hunger,
and weakness. I hate it —

the weakness and hovering. I push out
my hand, ancient weapon. But too late.
The word's begun to fill with blood.

The Door

What are you expected to do, wish for
a small break or a big win?

It's not enough to stare, you can't
always tell from this distance, the car
moves too quickly, the rain recalibrates
so does street noise.

Something woke you last night
and it wasn't bad thoughts
you leave that to others wiser, more beautiful
who understand popularity and language
but maybe not the allusions.

And maybe birds, too, fly by as soon as
you think about the door.

You think about the door all the time.

Inside and Outside Houses

To move slowly at the bench
and cupboards of a lit-up kitchen,
to watch a woman do this
and then walk on. To turn
into a narrow street that falls
down the hill to docks, tangled lines
of cranes, carriages, cargo,
night spark of the city
across the bay.

To see the moon from a back window,
netted by branches of bare trees,
to be aware that people notice the moon
looking up from their preparations,
to walk on quicker, to prevent contact
disturbing the slow, soft air,
early brush of winter evening.
To unload shopping from an opened car,
to rub fur and whiskers against a tyre,
a kind of greeting, caress of ownership,
to leave a trace, to move on
leave black cat and bending man
with the weight and light of home.

To feel the moon behind my shoulder now,
steady, clear in a colder region
above the deep routine of evening
inside and outside houses,
quiet movement of this suburb on a planet.

To be glad the next gate is my own.

Milky Way Poem

The stars are there.
We go out
to see them
and say they are out
until we grow cold
and go in.
The stars are there.

Things I Learned In Bay 13A

That sleep is imagination and I was immaculate
within a hangar of flowers, but there's no time for food.
A kind of leverage is essential when sheets attract blood
and that accompanying shot of salt.
That youth falls off its stem, though rays of fraud
still promise the thought of juggling desires.

It's all about how your water runs
and how it's accepted on the charts, the noisy gauge
the stethoscope, that loss may be indistinguishable
in the day and a purged dial tone is normal.

What is scary, if the darkness that is being cannot die
nor will it change, though all are changed?
Despite chameleons breathing into ether, I find that
on this graph the image of my heart is there.

.

That sleep is a contract of itself although beauty
isn't right anymore, the cannula blooms a tattoo
within the shadow of my inner arm, how easy it is
to repeat 'British Constitution' when there is none.
That I know I'm here because today is any day, 1st of Feb
and unfortunately I know the prime minister's name.

Voiceless flowers throw out their odour between
the grossly sterile and a body's dutiful stench
the pressure of feet and agitated clips of papers
the incandescence of the asterisk.

A shed flower lies where water doesn't work, outside
there's no southerly nor change, the soft rope cries
I was the lucky dream, 'out of here', and on the script
how more machines will make my image there.

.

That sleep is neither fantasy nor sensible.
It is a shed flower that balances then falls to the left-
hand side, the sharp pleasure is a phantom
with a ruinous smile, but time seems a relative
of nobody here. There's a sideshow of blips and bings
on the monitors and the azure curtains take their turn
in each act of rays through crosshairs
onto hefted and wrapped glass plates.

Like understudy revenants in unknotted gowns, we're
waiting for some allegro of welcome breeze, a miracle
like air's sky blue, or cake, to multiply our breathing
with my slow heart, boom boom, they attempt to find delays
in the desiring damp of my jiggy pulses
as if looking inward I'd find my picture there.

Self and Nothingness

I'm running all over the world. I'm running
within sight of what might happen.
I'm running with a crazy kind of make-do.

The new plants waver in cold evening.
It's cooler than when I left these things, these ideas
in rooms. Is there a knack to it?

If I could shift my head without the world
shifting. It can't be that hard to look up
into the trees. I know they're there.

I've argued over silence.
I've collected nonsense.
I crave nothingness.
I know it doesn't exist.
That it does.
I am a source of virtual violence.

What senses are, I'm not sure, or how many.
I smell strange but that could be
the way air is.

The craft is the devil, disquiet a relief
jokes become bullet points, and my life
an account explained in columns.

Perhaps the essence has dissolved, become paler.
Whether to drink it, whether to pour it
whether to watch something else drink it.

Perhaps it's all a set-up. It doesn't matter
what it is. Everything in my mouth
cracks like a sweet.

I am a project as I scour the streets, for
what it's worth, and I'm looking for ways
to write back the damage.

I'm Almost Good

My goddess part has deserted me, though I watch stars
over my shoulder. It makes me dizzy.

My heart's white as copy paper
waiting for my next lie.

My bones are almost as tired as my skin.
My skin is too tight to think.

I am half-elegy, or a half-chewed sweet.

I collect dust but only certain dust.
No, I won't tell you that secret.

I wake when I sleep
and don't know where I am.

This is normal.

I disposed of some junk. I talked through something epic.
Really, it seemed almost good.

I'm skirting the hours. I can't put anything into them.
I can't grasp even the seams of minutes.

I could walk over myself, if I wasn't so tired.

But I look as though I'm meant to be here
doing something important.

I don't need anyone's permission
to speculate that something's breaking.

I know everything is woe
and there's loud carriage in my head.

The timetable almost clicks into place.
The stories almost sound true and present.

Still, outside the window a honeyeater sings.
So does the city's traffic.

Above, there's a pressure of clouds
pretending to a storm front.

No-one's fooling anyone.
It's tense, it's not great.

No wonder I lean on the fence
as if it's the place to be.

Here's the gate, there's the road.
And now the rain, the wet ground. That pitch!

Really, it seems almost good.

from Little Whirling Songs

Dust Spring Late

late spring
dust late sprite
dust late spring duty
late spruce dyke
late dye
sprint late dust
sprinkle late dynamite sprout
late spring dawdle
late sprocket
dust late spring
dynamo late springs late
too late spring
to dust

Oh, Wait! Decisions

Are dinners like clues
Are defects like charms
Are deeds like characters

Are dragons like concepts
Are departures like choirs
Are destinations like claims

Are diaries like cliffs
Are dolls like competitions
Are ducks like configurations

Are echoes like consumers
Are eggs like continuities
Are embarrassments like conversions

Live, Loop, Lop

The eternal return goes routine
   and I'm living on the doll.
The eternal return goes rubbish
   and I'm loaning out the dolphin.
The eternal return goes rugby
   and I'm loopy on the downs.
The eternal return goes rugged
   and I'm logging on the double.

The eternal return does a runner
   and I'm lopping off the dominance.

Cool Night Refrain

learn a languish   send off your poverty

lax & lax   without timing or sweeping

     splash!

After Memoriams

Closing time debates the
patterned pain nor can
songs necessary whisper
always write horizon
travelling and currents.

Take better joy.
Take water's thousand.
This book of night stings
over wrack into my mind
can set new travelling
thus hard true.

The Slide

Sometimes they put you in seas
or rivers without telling you.
The river is dark, let's say
and trees are low over you.
In the branches are owls
making noises like a machine
breathing.

After you come away from this
you have a scar and a jar
where you swim.
It is chemical, archaeological
and violent.

So you wash it all away.
It's too early for things to be
broken or twisted
but even when you run, you fall.

All your life, if you could fly
all your life slides from under you
and you do not have to swallow
water or hear it.

You do not have to but you must
as the clouds fall without telling you.

Some (   ) Time

fragile tears or strong enough falling
all
that's left
the uncertain lengths

there are possibles, rain on earth
lacunae
and lostness
but are everywhere

and to hear crackles of diodes
think
of a
few recovered scraps

ardent/ ears/ eyes the taste, skin
some future time——
will think
?

ache in time along with leaves

— with a fragment from a fragment of Sappho

In Air

Move slowly and compose in air
Your mind walks with ghosts on the ceiling

Stand as you move into your limbs
Love your fences and stone as you may

There's no reply that won't hurt you

Do, Make, Steal, Sing

Waver on stilts while listening to arias.

Sew your own rose and ask of its questions.

Steal flotsam like wanton flies.

Ruin lyrics, while above the egrets lift.

Paste green language around a cork room.

Refuse to 'nail it'. Just refuse.

Keep rearranging what is footnote and what is space.

Walk out one day in presences.

Take night's immediate nerve with possibility.

Speculate outside with the big southerly.

Pass as you go into.

Sleep all around at blue windows.

Burn down the villa, change all the doors.

Stand so shadows make you perfect.

Love your dumb corpus, of song.

6.

*Not as straight as the wall
but standing, taller*

(The new poems)

'I can look — can't I —'

Please go with me
   even through this
province of want
where we're between
   beyond and disquiet
the kissing wind
   from the north
is longing and flits
like unconscious company
   its music tugs

Hey all you little sound spirits
clicking through night
   hello cupboards
smelling of clothes
   cups bread
cotton tin
   and cinnamon
moss is winter's hassock

Nothing is minor   but small
   things tremor
barefoot
   and careful
infinite close heartbeat
   quick as my arm
o comrade moment at the door
time to rise

And the World is Breath

I set sail every morning
  unhooking day from night
The window is a breath
The north is scudded
  with patches of white
A cloud is a breath

Not all days have clouds
  but here they are
The passing train is a breath
A cold wind blows
  over the summer
The fallen nest is a breath

Every return is a pattern
  one map undoes another
I stare into a clear dark sky
  as planes fly across
    night in a diagonal
The interrupted dream is a breath

I'm wandering with ghosts
  against screens and machines
There are no clouds
The sky seems to be humming
A receipt from an auto-teller
  is a breath

The air is full of leaves and wind
  but no clouds
A parking space is a breath
A gum tree against

the clear blue seen
  from the bus is a breath

Memory is every breath
Ghost clouds float
  in the hot blue
    above the parklands
Every second is for something
Forgetting is another breath

The Full Present

Perhaps memory is a kind of remedy
or an aching sea

I try to open each jar, each box
each old minute again

It's almost as if night will
overturn me

Remembering makes you ancient, I think
My cells, I think, are lying

I listen to the old songs
You can still get them replayed

I misremember years

A date can be a lie
that wind and rain say constantly

Just as love is difficult to prove
there's only the present, which is stolen

Perhaps saying has all been said
into the humid blank night
full only with the moon

And the dead
who are always too quiet

St Petersburg

I nearly got to St Petersburg
I sailed out towards the Baltic

I tried to call you through the shimmer
(Remember the ferry sailing past the low rocky islands)

There were news reports of a Russian sub in the archipelago — I said —
The clouds were maps of what was coming — you said —

Everyone went crazy with accusations — I said —
Up there the infinities sneak through — you said —

Later a tiny one-man sub sailed into Sickla Canal — I said —
We were going along too easily — you said —

Did you get my messages — I said —
The clouds are always there, hard to read — you said —

The future's a beautiful hope, inside and outside time
It's why we nearly got to St Petersburg

Pretty Vacant

A reluctance, almost a reluctance
A relying
A surgery and a queue
Antibody quarrel
An output no blisters
But why is it when it isn't

A remains or a surplus
A chamber with no voltage
Outrageous placebo
No database
Soiled as quaintness
But why isn't it beautiful when it is

A remnant, almost a remnant, any remnant
A centrist with no visa
A single surfboard
No blondes no seesaws
A quid and a syllable of anxiety
But why are the surroundings outrageous if they're not

A synthesis in anticlimax
A certainty of no visit
A remedy, almost a remedy
Antecedents and more accounting
Anything vacant
But why is there a downturn when there's a downpour

Why is it
Vacant
Remnant
Soiled

(with)
Reluctance

Gone In Terrain

An eagle looks like time
                 then flies above it
flight movement and colour lost
         within ranges
    perpetual light   perpetual fall
weathered roadside shadows
     as the never-ending begins
              world of cloud and crosswinds.

The bird flies out of sight
             and the myth
is still everlasting
     that we will taste this air
       as day sweat or
           a later moon to cry under.

And home lines end in becoming
     wood returns to land
       as cracks run through us
years slant across patterns in walls.

In silence is no silence   or sounds our feet make
     in ruins where
         desperate
          ancient
           water
tracks down walls
     disappears as a saint weeps
         into plaster
    the adept oxidisation of ages
       sacrifice
eccentric ultimate bones

a lasting feathery pattern
        under hollow windows.

Or as if some ghost
        exploded gaps in pug and pine
an unlucky toss
        of galvo crashed on ground
           with old gear
           and paraphernalia
among undone magic of brick and iron
        even doors have lost their shadows.

Ecstasies of heat touch us
        igniting morning
           a pattern of nests angle in a tree
smoothness and dryness   death in branches
                death just barely below
this old firmament
        embrace of white stones and ochre.

Sand runs like the water this once was
        as memory folds bodies back
into their field of mulch
        as ground speaks in hum
about how we've wrecked time.

        Did anyone ask the country
           did anyone ask
                anyone?

Sun and water make colours
        what you craft
           out of the singing moment
        articulate hush

pulsing in tracks and fences
        how clouds fill at this angle
           with a faint orange.

Thought percolates into thought
    the air's material
        dust and sound
            changing direction
passing wheels
    the last curve
        of the earth.

Sky is inexorable
    becomes
        almost
           anything.

Nothing is
        ever finished.

All Shook Up

We're sliding on the corrugated crust
of colony, its shipwrecks, its bushfire plans,
its road kill, the sound of the plastic sea.
There's lizard twigs on a dirt road
the air's full of time zones, rustling through
heathlands, sliding into the gulf
along with fossils and cigarette butts.
We're watching bushland shimmering
in sea breeze, everything's a tide.

You can believe in something beautiful
that's passing, a large male roo
in the middle of the road stares us down
turns away to the bush on the slope.
My bones are separating, the car's suspension
holds, only just, we slip on laterite
and the moment, there are only moments, then
everything's gone, again, from here
the sea's almost clear and blue in the shallows.

There's nothing we can do
even with a camera, even with words.
Further south there's Antarctica.
Well, we hope it's still there.
Hope is what we have, which does nothing.
Clouds move above, they're still around,
white on blue, sky tides, sure.
The past isn't the present isn't
the future, so if someone foresaw this
they may wake soon.

West Bay, Kangaroo Island

The Sky Is The Great Entrance

What is the world of breath?
The air is a huge forest blowing

Is matter always in flight?
Everything bends with love but can't be folded in a box

Was I once a sea, a very small one?
Every night is the morning of my death and my resurrection

How often have I floated so that I could rise?
All sounds end with sky and ocean

What kind of magic is rain?
I am the dust of an asteroid, the blink of an atom passing
another

Aren't all corners special?
Here are the great laws of photosynthesis, volume, gravity

What is the dark matter of love?
The endless turning atmosphere, the shaping wind

Where is the sky's origin or end?
Air is gold with starlight when I step out towards the sand

What is it about rending that seems sad, isn't that a kind of
making?
As if this underworld was clear and cool, or a place to hide

How often has my breath caught on my body?
Matter in the end is always light

Isn't time a kind of detour, but necessary?
The dust of others, waves of grass

Isn't every discussion an unravelling?
There's this assonance in things   waves   tracks   days

Is it here you stop making sense?
Crows circle above the shuddering trees

Elsewhere Here

1.
What is the colour
of the world?
The bush flame?

And how should I begin?

With phantoms
like portents
a blowtorch on the roadhouse
the pity blues
dogs don't let up bragging.

In the aftertaste of mourning
are bankrupt sermons 'twit twit twit'

as the blackbird's
night trade sharpens
into sorrow.

J'écrivais des silences, des nuits, je notais l'inexprimable.

What sound
is without fault?

Nocturnes harangue
or bluff the summer's morale.

I no longer have any excuse
for epigrams but they trail behind me.

Each time the coda crumbles
my ligaments seize.

The sound of floorboards mocks me.
The house of labour

turns me loose.
I am the trouble of what I write.

2.
Phantoms from treetops
fall like footprints
the brightness delaying
as beginnings do.

It's a disagreement with time
and the place of things.
A diurnal shimmer.

Noon melts into darkness.
I wrote silences and nights

We're preoccupied or helpless.
Hectic broadcasts and think tanks
are the only conversation.

Is sound our fault?

Is there some other source, a charm
a new style we swing on a catwalk
like a charlatan with his magical stutter
with prescriptions for elsewhere.

Something grabs me in passing
a syllable, a sound that becomes one word then another.

I recorded the inexpressible

This isn't retreat but utterance
over ego, and the fierce doors of this house

turn my trouble loose.

3.
Eucalypt litters
daydream.

The summer night sky
turns into view.

Buds have become moments.

Flowerbeds spread
sunshine's rattle.

Pollen begins to drown
and there's a syllabic noise on the breeze.

Each new dream twitches
like a green stem.

We break, we slide, we shift.
We have secret loves
we hide away
in poems.

A kind of sanctuary
a kind of tolerance
a charge on the soul (if that's what you call it).

It feels like whiplash or a liquor never brewed
a springboard, a new enzyme, desire

that drags you out of spasms in your sinews.
It's not a fault of sound, but a beginning

once begun continues without too much mockery.
lets every irony echo

— there is nothing that is just one —

Just as dawn chorus is not one. Even
single things rescue each other

and elsewhere is also here.

Salt Water Kin

As water turns & returns   it changes from
    ocean   ground   & sky   onto
these beachside rocks   as I taste salt water
    kin of saliva   (a memory of exploring rock pools)

I look into today's pools   they're swirled clear
    or gathered with irritant   like pearl

as surge catches in sandstone   sings hollows
    where submerged grasses weep
posidonia sinuosia   heterozostera tasmanica

*

What is a wave but a moment   & a continuum
    in wordless language   swell   pitch   break
shaping its cold sweat on our cars   our skin
    as the city rolls into the gulf   abandoned water bottle
in the tide's reach

*

Stray sky water falls on my cheek
    the truest fragment may be a rain drop
even if not transparent   it carries so much
maybe some days are grey for a reason

as this present fills up with pasts   sea past
    bird past   fish trails   rain history   in clouds
vapour   brine   erosions   cinders of trees & ice

tasting bitter   like everything we've had to swallow

like crust   of the pink lake we once passed
     clapped out memory of a green shore   slurries &
shams hunched on cracked industrial edges

*

The sea has no nostalgia   its currents
     undo everything   strew & scrape   leavings
of the extinct   some things fresh

icecream wrapper   old bricks turned to pebbles
     new washed shells   plastic in forever colours
worn wood   cuttle bone

Today, seagulls steal garbage from our hands
we shout   'hey, here'   by the lagoon
     sandhills   the pier   as landscapes stretch
from us   watery   dry   across the world

Will the clear water return?

*

Until everything silts up   this is what we do
     cup water to our mouths   & spill it
     for ground   write in this salt   fresh   tongue
turn over its ancient syllables   without drowning

Hope For Whole

No!   No boom-town   no brown current
no smoky vessel   no swollen cooked mud
no slop shock   no money juggle
no ghost bloom   no blunt petrol hull
no smudge rock   no possess.
Yes!   Keep the lode under.
Hope for old flows to grow
polyp   sponge   weed
rock   mollusc
worm   turtle   dugong.

Conserve, do not stress.
Love the blue levels
the upwell   the fluent spheres under
guyot   gull sweep   storm hover
sky green fluxes   fresh flume.
Defend exoskeletons   broken hydro-forest.
Stop runoff   overuse.
Don't cut holes under clouds.
You new crown-of-thorns, go!
No short-term clever
no smoke-burn genus murder.
Begone!

Keep us hold whole.
Let enfold of
north to south
whole blue current
whole source   flush blood
mother cells.
Hope for whole country
not those who would strop

or cull reef.
Keep touch the swell deep course.

Contains no 'a' or 'i' vowels — no Adani.

River: Contra/indications

Even if I see and don't see the river's writhing
the fish   daphnia   algae   the water   the water
the swelling of   ritalin   warfarin   methotrexate

Even if I bend or don't bend to the flow   ingest
bitter tasting wonders as do aquatic insects   riparian spiders
soaked in   memantine   codeine   fluconazole   mianserin

Even if the nerve system of antidotes flushes me with tics
'Platypuses feed on the insect larvae that live on the creek bed'
aggression   numbness   memory loss   unwanted rules of the algorithm

> Past the old flux of   apoplexy   breakbone   dropsy   grief
> grippe   horrors   jaw-faln   lethargy   lockjaw   nostalgia
> palsy   quinsy   rickets   scurvy   spleen

Even if I know it's too much and not enough 'with ageing
infrastructure there's some leakage'   with my own sweet body   is all
I offer   baptismal slough of   perfume   cologne   skin   lotion   sunscreen

Even if the nerve system of doses will cure my blurred vision
steroids move from cows to waterways through banks
and sediments   tiredness   aches   anaemia   unusual bruising

Even if my nerve system splits from its diminishing returns
silent and hardened   destroyed   duplicitous and   dumb
I'm not quite lost though I may not speak up

In that plagued flux   dying still navigates living
welcome stone-fly larvae   leafy twig-rush   all you tiddlers
everything as part   of things   nothing to rule earth   but little ones

A Trodden Morning

Would it be better if there were no dollars?
If it wasn't a question. If exchange could drift.

We'd still rise in air, the sun, as though
we hadn't paid for all this, pockets, excess.

That we'd gambled all our proteins, see, a packet
falls like a branch and we watch numbers grow.

The bees are productive. They're not concerned with
standards or how a malaise spreads up our necks.

We step out into the nation. No, we live with it
that is, with our shoulders but can't see our hands.

Television or streaming don't bind us like they used to
as portals offering freedom, the instruction kit, the glimpse.

Our mysteries are warmer, dodging between the frost.
To be sentient, a little tinny, with things we can't pay for.

Flight Matter

A wing is harder than air

There are ghosts in the air

They sound like birds but how

Ghosts have no sound

It's too hard to sing across the border

Easier to fly straight into matter

A page's matter is its sound

It isn't perfect, not like a bird

It's not perfect like flight

Neither is it a revenant nor is it pretending

Neither is a bird pretending

If ghosts are sounding, is it a song for a bird, or for me

A torn page flutters like a wing in hard air

This air blows into each word in any world

The Scatter Singing

River you step in   a road
Direction litters
in different ways outside   my head

Thank you air, why
I'm here
Thanks dust   all you burials, roads
rocks, the sea   recumbent obstacles

Relax!
Lasting moments   are only moments
    in gardens, on nature strips
I never learned to ride a bike

The colours of things   always change
universal   like the galaxy
You can see some of it
from here on a clear night

Or birds resting in wetlands
How long have they been here?
I don't know   hiding so much

You little dinosaurs of flight
You ancient soundings
And you rightly scatter from me

    Yet, singing

As Omens

Am I none but a habit
Circling in a madrigal of lungs
    And flowers heaving into the air
        Diatribes and buttonholes

Is heat now a given
    Or a dash to the back fence
Everyone's a honey
    Trying to sound modern
As the articulate order freaks out
In its husky polyphonics

Treatments can be loud
As omens from the forest or the street
Curtains open onto silence
    An unseen child   weeping light
        A messenger from the dead

The prowess of devils lies
    In their woo and their tendrils
As our sweet seams undo
Into this stunned region of matter
    Bring your products and your hooks

Yes, the underworld is outside
    Listening   the laughing stars
Pause at the fence   in the deranged dawn
    Who will pay

What to turn off
    The moon
Or the next day

These Truths

I am in bed with worry
grasping at the real
while dawn flexes
its magpie

somewhere
out there
a school girl drives
a car into a barricade

will it make the news who
makes the news
about pickets or bricks
the violence of shares

those things in my ear
a truth syrup
not answering
fresh grief

Seen

Or show me another thing I've never yet seen
like nippers and hikers watching for bombs.
Maybe there are too many oligarchs
and globes for them to care who wins.
Show me how railway stations flinch
at midnight when seeds are homeless.
Tell me about those marshlands emptied of
alphabets, slinking untold into another bereft sea.

Show me how agnostic you've had to be
amongst almshouses and heathens, how easy it is
to fill your workshop with more clangers,
to slop on your wastelands and one-time saints.
Show me your brights and detachments, your old
fashioned faxes, remind me of chalkdust and wasps.
Show me an almanac where we still may appear.
I don't need a weatherman or any more luminaries.

Call me when your uprights are gone, let me thread
another transgression, then rearrange labyrinths,
empty the synthetics, douse the detectors,
and hold you above salt-free technocrats.
Then I'll undo the synods, the bonfires, the statesmen.
Paris is rusting, and London bursts with machines.
Come south, here are the swoops and sediments.
Be my irritant amongst all the clampdowns.

Unbuttoned

If I have to earn some skin
does it have to be new?
Can I recycle my mother's
wedding dress, a gallon of blue paint,
the leftover hotel shampoo?
Maybe there's also something
around me I should return,
the coat I stole from winter
back east, my old feathers,
or the scales I can't remember
growing in the afternoon.
But, yes, there's the photograph,
me in a skewed school hat,
oversized boots looking green
in light coming through
the window covered in its skin
of last century's flowers.
There's that weird glimmer of hope
or fantasy that now itches
along with the lies I told,
archives falling from my hair,
those ribbons that never stayed put.
If I have to earn some other coat
do I need to still keep warm?
Or shall I unbutton and fold
what's left, step out of my nerves
and my veins, leave everything
— corpse, crevice, carcass, shell —
but keep my breath for
the impending and tremendous air
that's beyond howling when
I touch it to my old pelt?

Wandering as Method

I thought of that city, a place I couldn't have foreseen.
Your unknown arms formed along its infinite.

See how I filter my blindness, as though it strains
to the very thought of you, as one who's never been
visualised amongst all this flash. You were silence. Words
may wink, each sentence make its small advance.

Can I really not pretend, lever not one single detail
with such nerve, such savoir faire, a wish to please
this damaged love, this viral, unnecessary god.

From our garden the zeal had poured away
so I don't remember why we started.
Broken breath revealed the white wound beneath.

I purified my heart with courage and indifference.
I wander in my doubter's method of the way.

Bending the Frame

A red door has never stopped anyone.
It's better to hide in the curves.

White surfaces are full of obscurities.
Perpendiculars aren't easy under a roof.

The corner is rough, where you go tripping.
The broken handle, who can fix it?

Inside is entwined, and doubled by between.
It's hard to read the sunlight.

Shadows have their own colours.
Walls fuse with doubts.

Windows can almost be companions.
The yellow floor is trembling.

Am I bending the frame by asking?
The terrace is indigo and matches the night.

Some space is a relief.

— *after Spatial Composition 4, Katarzyna Kobro*

Space is Blue in Being

Space is blue as morning
as noon, as evening
At midnight the dark forest parts for you

Our mouths are space
our craniums, wombs
the air tunnelling songs through our lungs

Space is where all space lives
it broods near its edges
darker and more vehement as it swells

Space has spoken, you can hear it
where you are, where you will be
There's nothing more primary than here

Light lifts its corners
where space becomes space again
and all colour is stretching like a tree

Space is a window, a shining
a murmuring screen
green as heaven, blue as the underworld

Lift your grassy tongue into the dark
hear how your feet walk through each space
how blue they become

— *after Space, Dušan Marek*

Composed of Light
For Clarice Beckett

The world's so close,
you touch its breath
  spirit matter   the body
working at a table yet
weightless almost, without
grandeur

Colours and fresh air
hand you the materials
canvas, bristles, the world
of the bay, the city
a refraction
transcendent as sunset
through clouds
a packet from the pantry
clatter in a sink

The sympathies are
shivering brightness, passing cars
your feet escaping on gravel

Consolation
to be windblown
or tremble in a day's passing
through all light's colours

  restless light
  resonant light   composed light
  equivocal light   light perpetual

Infinite colour
falls from your hands
companion solace of
long working hours

How much
    do we need   to love
    the world?

— after 'Sunset', Clarice Beckett

Poem With a High Wind Blowing Over It From the East

It blows leaves around
like letters —
forms shapes to-
gether

in highs and lows
I can't read
I'm distracted
scatter and branch

by voices a cloud
that's now dis-
appearing

We need clouds —

I watch kids bowl
at the nets
serious / accurate
'line and length' —

A small dog sniffs me —
feet to knees —
I think I pass

At the corner I dodge
a yellow tripod —
'it's a boundary
survey' says the guy
levelling a theodolite

'Aim the crosshair
in the viewing scope
at the point
to be measured'

Boundaries linger
even if fences fall —
I'll be trespassing soon
with or without strong measure

The east wind is hot
and doesn't care
kisses me as it passes
and yes I let it

— again and again

I will not be forgiven, I will not repent

Is Anyone Anonymous?

I'm a real girl an illusory girl
   hot at the microphone
      Imagine!

I collapse after timetables
The moon changes its hat
Not everything's noble

There's a rhythm
   at the window like hunger
as if there's noise inside the future
   an ancient tone
      a crotchet of silence

My clothes avoid surveillance
I'm incongruent
   and between algorithms

I pick a page in a book
read the signs
arise from there
   into the medicated air
full of space and small affinities

Rain drops tunes of the season
into the machine of early light
   its tenderness more casual
than any dream of talking to
   fishes has-beens or escapees
on the suburb's horizon
where people drop their shoes

And there are still tongues
  like comebacks or an aria
that proceeds slowly
  out of a piano
    in a front room

An Address To The Shadow That Follows Me

I'm still your goddess of crumbs and scraps, chewing on suburban air
Let me tell you, it takes some guts to do that
amongst these pokerfaced love shacks and villa clones

I scour the darkness like a cute machine
Tell me, am I stubbornly retro and trashy in my dreams
or just curled up with portents and movie themes

I am not convinced by bargain bins, html, pantyhose
nature strips, auto-tune, or the next kitsch theory

I am not a theory
I am where I lay my dead

Should I wander elsewhere, a country called Freedonia
the lower east side of Middle Earth, the northern suburbs
of circumstance, amongst the daffodils

Shall I rise and become strange blue milk at dawn
or simple and rhythmic as the train to the city
Morning drapes on the fence as I stand in the doorway's never

Remember when we used to do things
Time was a spider web, a new leaf, clitoral shadow
Now hours are suspended in my giddy rooms

The light sings in the ceiling, why do all these rooms change places
I'm clutching cords, folds and batteries as a way to steady things
In the end I'm meat, a minor character in a cli-fi novel

Should I go make some history, like a snake, the Red Sea
sputnik, or Trelawney scrabbling in hot sand for Shelley's

    unburned heart
Even while I photocopy the past, my ears hum like stars

Let me tell you, there are places
where even you cannot follow me, where I can no longer go

As I walk into the sun, where are you, back there
with all the shadow friends, my shadow, friend

Being Changed

I am sap
breathtake
sound of
another day
a little door
swinging
with breezes

looking for
a superpower
in this implacable
taxed body

like all our
devices
sending signals
emojilike
to impossible
objects thinking
we shall
be changed
in the twinkling
of a text

immortality
like the seconds
of haunting
before sleep

Atmosphere

I can't wish on stars in unseasonal cold.
They're older than they look.
And they keep shtum in shivery night
even when I sneak up on them.
Still they spread a stern and spiky glow
on my uneven thinking about
how things turned out, horizon
to horizon, birth to dust.

All that dust is real, it floats eternally
and there you are or will be, or perhaps
you were, flickering from atmosphere
to atmosphere.

You don't have to say a word
and, of course, you can't.
I pretend the birds do that for you.
I pretend the stars effervesce
or mean something like a portent
when all I look at is the past while
trees are still busy, and the late traffic.
You're going somewhere too.

I Must Constantly Be in Motion Even Standing Still

The words for fear and run for stay and hold
all loop through my sinews each and every

Kissed by breath and tongue

That forms then flies as if being a bird

Might save me

Every word knows how to turn as I'd run down the street who will

Believe me even if I shout

Every song is about loss
and about this road I'm keeping on

Knowing what I learn won't save me and what I say

Is a cloud in a valley is a storm on the hills is the way
someone pushes you around in a corridor

My muscles and pores still say what they knew

How being exposed must feel

I'm not every woman but I believe in windows getaways
keeping a pencil with me like a weapon as if the only
news that *is* the news could be scribbled on my tongue

To announce a word a kiss into air
bearer of light of water of what's made of from words

A vowel is the way breath moves through the mouth

A consonant interrupts

What's trying to be said is here and gone, at teeth, lips
tip of my tongue   Or yours

Fragmenta Nova: 16 Views of a Day

this woven heat, this crown
    of heavy scented   toil, to walk, to arrive
           under a scud of clouds   air I hear across my face

each branch bears light and drops over the hours   a car skids
    it's a form of cleansing   clear mid-blue sky

all day, all day moving around streets, the rooms   we all shoulder
                                              goods

I find old words   words that have passed in mouths
          or listen for syllables in the breeze
                that makes a pattern   in endless ribbons

time is imprinted in work and detritus
      leaf and thorny twig   the tug of light

this day, each day I dwell inexactly with the dead of my dream life
    all rooms fill with echoes   that's the thing about walls

I fall over a chair   I stare at the chair   the chair does nothing
                                that's its genius

clouds drift in again and a cold breeze travels my skin

pink evening light
      who can decipher the birds?
          they flower out   burst in lines and arcs

now is cricket time as well   evening song
        there's a dog somewhere   sounding anxious

take this coat   unwind its graceful
        aged sleeves from my arms   to relax now
    but do I ease?   o chair, o table

I crackle around minutes   the thorny ideas
        I sit with a meal   you ask me
                I scour my memory
                        I scrape a plate   push an idea further

I wait for the meteor shower   nothing falls that we can see

the body has its own space all night   this is what pain tells us
        this   leaf-crowned window
                        sends out its signal

and why I'm sleep-pierced with old dreams
            tomorrow's a full moon   full of ghosts

the curtains lap up each minute

Little Heartbeats

I don't know anything
about blue &
gusts play around birds

Jasmine these days
is a co
incidence

Obstinacy — red
as summer's
dirty secret

Hair keeps growing &
I float
in tide

.

My nerves —
threading windows
Give me the map!

The browsing cure-all
only covers
so much

I wonder what is
length & rain
is deeper in afternoon

Should I
gush all the love &
stop frowning

.

Help me Venus!
I know you're up there
in the busy stars

A luxuriant gamble —
the dictionary at 3am
into the yellow yonder

I'm working
on the fly as a
friend of night

Three words watch me —
book, bowl, window
above any purpose

Fate is a Virus

how my hair has fallen
over the world of my feet, over
splatter, my pallor, my loves, my cheek

I hunger for undergrowth, unsaved junk
mudflats, alarmed confessions, rain as a ghost feast
it doesn't hate you   necessarily

the streets in the suburb are everlooping
funkish form fumbles on a twirl, a shame shag

even dogs speak in bitcoin whack
modern ecstasies sling round the supermarket
from cha-cha palace to bitch slap

online dalliance slopes over conspiracies
wish bent leaning into forever wherever
the stars went

The Names On My Breath

I've exchanged my names in doorways
I've buried them, recited them
dropped them from a cliff as echoes

I've unbuttoned them in the quiet, sorted them
into leaves, carried them like silvery traces
coins, barter, old currencies, analogue entrails

My breath is name saying same and also
shifting, a pattern undoing, a garden left
to weather, broken fences, mites, worms, birds
whatever the planet has to say when it hears me

In the night I don't have my name
It escapes, treading carefully through syllables
and starlight, an unread text in its pocket

I catch the one you give me or what a dream
gives me, the one I can't interpret, the one
that knows me

Each letter of these names has its own time
then exits   that old breath forming
the moment of a name, that singular forgotten one
as it unfurls

Acknowledgements

The section quotes are from poems in my first two books that are not included here:

The Mask and the Jagged Star
2. 'It is impossible to live as if we are free', from 'Fire on the harbour'
5. 'it's a long time since I've come home this way', from 'Cruising on a ridge of silence'
6. 'Not as straight as the wall / but standing, taller', from 'Around the White Vase'

Flagging Down Time
1. 'I'm on my way under clouds / which don't let anything escape / (you have to deal with it)', from 'There's knowledge and then the sky'
3. 'clear, grey light falls forever, / over the other side — the horizon', from 'Balancing on darkness'
4. 'the way the air touches you, if it's free or heavy', from 'The power of a room'

The collected poems in this book were selected from the following books:

The Mask and the Jagged Star, Hazard Press, 1992 (NZ)
in the distance on the verandah
mother i am waiting now to tell you
The Phantom Division

Flagging Down Time, Five Islands Press, 1993
Maria Callas is With Me Tonight
When Planets Softly Collide
Inside and Outside Houses

The Book of Possibilities, Hale & Iremonger, 1997

Jazz and Stars
The Pure in Heart
The Kitchen Light
Disrepair
Where the Sea Burns
Antipodean Geography

Screens Jets Heaven: New and Selected Poems, Salt Publishing 2002 (UK)
Marrickville Sonnet
Train in Vain
Futurism at Night
Screens, Jets, Heaven
The Night Before Your Return
A Taste for Hunger

Broken/Open, Salt Publishing, 2005 (UK)
The Skim
Refrains on Sand
Displacements
The Mini Series
from Struggle and Radiance: Ten Commentaries
Where Wind Falls
Winged
Sea and Star
from Limits We've Shouldered
The New Aesthetic
Heat in a Room
Grass
To Sleep Inside Rain
Fractures
The Dissolve

Dark Bright Doors, Wakefield Press, 2010
O Fortuna

All Night, All Night
Sorry I'm Late
Mystery Train
Waking Alone By the Radio
Leaving it to the Sky
Seeds
The Thought of an Autobiographical Poem Troubles & Eludes Me
Figure
Night Visitor
Dreaming Homeward
The Green Dress

Ash is Here, So are Stars, Walleah Press, 2012
from Where We Live
A Moon Song
Whose Words Did These Things?
Brilliant Slippy Works
Blue Lines
All Blues
A Time to Refrain from Embracing
While All This is Going On
Tracking
I Must Be With You in the Cold Time
from My Fugitive Votive

The Beautiful Anxiety, Puncher & Wattmann, 2014
The Beautiful Anxiety
Wave
Misinterpretations /or The Dark Grey Outline
The Spare Winter
What's Coming Next
from My Ruined Lyrics
from Six Temperamental Sonnets
The Tender Stone

I am, I
The Dress Sonnet
La Vida Loca
Big Flower
The Slide
Some (   ) Time
In Air

Breaking the Days, Whitmore Press, 2016
Email is a Record
The Louder Silence
Dust and Ice
Shiver
Blossom
When the Green Starts
Happy Families
from The Plover in the Poem and What Meaning Does Not Mean
The Door
Milky Way Poem

Brink, Five Island Press, 2017
Big Apple Leaf Summer
Edge Against Sign
Blue
In My Shifts
Our Epic Want
Weed Grounds
Brushing Yonder
Wind Shadow
More Than Molecules
Everything is Beautiful, Finally
Mighty Tree
In This Wake
The Woodland Chapel

Afternoon Grey In
Self and Nothingness
from Little Whirling Songs
After Memoriams

Viva the Real, UQP, 2018
The End of May
The Quality of Light
Bitumen Time
Wrack
The Make-Do
The Storm
Poem Diesel Butterfly
Bohemian Rhapsody
Round Midnight
I am Brushing Myself
The Un-marvelling
An End of Flight
Let Loose Looks
Break on Through
Things I Learned In Bay 13A

A History Of What I'll Become, UWAP, 2020
This Crumbling Aura
Patience Without Virtue
The Doll and Me
Laundromat Near the Corner of Passage Alexandrine
Consummations
As Long as You Need / Fragments
What the Glass Holds
Oh Venus, That Zenith
These Things (braided)
Cursing Girl Gust
Mouth Form Flower

Touches / Touches Us
Into Our Thin Rivers
Elegiac Continuum
A Fantasia of Oddments, Wagers and Zeroes
Difficult Poem
Do, Make, Steal, Sing

Wild Curious Air, Recent Work Press, 2020
Deliberation on Sudden Days of Exceptional Brightness
The Moon, Antares, and the Dead As Well
I Walk as Jittery Mortal
Out of These Curves
The Vertigo Blues
A Piece of Everything
Wild Curious Air
I Welcome Night's Ruins
'It doesn't hurt to fall off the moon'
'I only wanted to see what the garden was like'
Possible Manners of Revelation
I'm Almost Good

These books are now out of print: *The Mask and the Jagged Star, Flagging Down Time, The Book of Possibilities, Screens Jets Heaven: New and Selected Poems, Broken/Open, Brink.*

These books are still available from their publishers, bookshops, or online sellers, as at mid-2023: *Dark Bright Doors, Ash is Here, So are Stars, The Beautiful Anxiety, Breaking the Days, Viva the Real, A History Of What I'll Become, Wild Curious Air.*

The new, ie. uncollected or unpublished poems, are all gathered into Part 6, the last part of the book, and thus are not listed again here. While a couple are unpublished, many others were first published, sometimes in different versions, in the following periodicals, and I would like to thank their editors for supporting this work: *Anthropocene* (UK), *Australian Poetry Journal, Blackbox Manifold* (UK), *The Brierfield Reader, Cordite Poetry Journal, foam:e, Ink Sweat and Tears* (UK), *Island, Meanjin, No Placebos, Orbis* (UK), *Overland, Plumwood Mountain, Rabbit, Red Room Poetry, The Saturday Paper, Shearsman* (UK), *Social Alternatives, Southerly, Stilts, The Suburban Review, The Warwick Review* (UK), *Westerly*.

'Salt Water Kin', was published in *Water Lore: Practice, Place and Poetics*, eds Camille Roulière and Claudia Egerer, London: Routledge, 2022 and subsequently in *Best of Australian Poems Vol 2*, eds Jeanine Leane & Judith Beveridge, Melbourne: Australian Poetry, 2022.

'Hope for Whole', was published in *Hope for Whole: Poets Speak up to Adani*, ed Anne Elvey, Rosslyn Avenue Productions in collaboration with *Plumwood Mountain*, 2018 (available as pdf).

'The Louder Silence' was set to music by Australian singer/ songwriter Jen Lush for an album of songs using poems by Australian poets, *The Night's Insomnia*, 2017. Her version of my poem was released as a youtube video. The album is available on Bandcamp and Spotify.

Notes on Poems

'The Moon, Antares, and the Dead As Well': The epigraph and the quoted phrase in the poem are from John Berger's book, *and our faces, my heart, brief as photos*. The poem also owes something to a reading of parts of Berger's book.

'Edge Against Sign': Every word or phrase in this poem also occurs across various poems in *The Mask and the Jagged Star*.

'Marrickville Sonnet': The lines from Petrarch can be translated as 'Through inhospitable and wild woods/ where armed men go at risk'.

'Where We Live': The sequence was first published as a collaborative work with photographer Annette Willis in the anthology, *The Material Poem*, ed James Stuart, available as a free download at: www. nongeneric.net/index.php?/publications/the-material-poem/.

'The Spare Winter': The line in quotes is translated from Du Fu.

'All Night, All Night': References the 2009 N1H1 swine flu virus pandemic.

'More Than Molecules': Owes a debt to Catullus, 48. The poem's epigraph is from that poem's final lines.

'Where Wind Falls': Includes a phrase based on a line from Lucretius, as used in Denise Riley's *The Words of Selves* (Stanford University Press, 2000).

'Futurism at Night': Uses the well-known phrase from Russian *Futuristy* proposals for a new language: *za/ um*, beyond/sense.

'I am, I': Composed entirely of phrases from poems by John Donne, 'Holy Sonnets'; Henry David Thoreau, 'I Am a Parcel of Vain Strivings Tied'; John Clare, 'I am'; Robert Herrick, 'The Vine'; Charles Simic, 'Prodigy'; Charles Wright, 'Homage to Claude Lorraine'; Trumbull Stickney, 'Fragment IX'; John Gay, 'The Beggar's Opera'; Amy Lowell, 'The Weather-Cock Points South'; Weldon Kees, 'For H.V.'; Robert Lowell, 'Mr Edwards and the Spider'; George Herbert, 'The Collar'; Ben Jonson, 'A Sonnet to the Noble Lady...'; Marianne Moore, 'Poetry'; Malcolm Lowry, 'Strange Type'.

'It doesn't hurt to fall off the moon': The poem's title quotes dialogue from the Jacques Rivette film, *Céline et Julie vont en bateau: Phantom Ladies Over Paris (Celine and Julie Go Boating)*, and it both directly and indirectly references some scenes in the film.

'Consummations': Consists of the three section break poems in *Brink*.

'As Long as You Need/Fragments': The poem is a series of mistranslations, misunderstandings, or loose versions of several fragments from Sappho.

'Cursing Girl Gust': *heofon* is Old English for 'the sky' or 'heaven'.

'Night Visitor': Recounts a waking dream about a visitation from a figure of Death, which I experienced a couple of times over a short period in the mid-1990s, and also relates to childhood dreams of being lost.

'I only wanted to see what the garden was like': The poem's title quotes from *Through the Looking Glass, and What Alice Found There* by Lewis Carroll. The poem itself was written after watching a documentary about the Argentinian poet, Alejandra Pizarnik, entitled *Alejandra* (dir. Ernesto Ardito, Virna Molina) and also refers indirectly to some of Pizarnik's poems and other writing.

'Things I Learned In Bay 13A': Bay 13A is, or was, one of the smallest curtained spaces in Sydney's Royal Prince Alfred Hospital Emergency Department. Patients who have experienced seizure-like symptoms are asked to name the Prime Minister and to repeat a number of phrases including 'British constitution'. My birth date is a 13th.

'I can look — can't I —': The poem's title is from Emily Dickinson's poem beginning with the words 'Good Morning — Midnight —' (also, and purely coincidentally, the title of a Jean Rhys novel).

'Elsewhere Here': Quotes 'And how should I begin?' from T.S. Eliot, 'The Love Song of J. Alfred Prufrock'; 'twit twit twit' from T.S. Eliot 'The Waste Land'; 'J'écrivais des silences, des nuits, je notais l'inexprimable.' from Arthur Rimbaud, 'A Season in Hell' (my version in English in section 2); 'a liquor never brewed' from Emily Dickinson, 'I taste a liquor never brewed'

'Hope for Whole': Adani Group is an Indian multinational conglomerate that, in 2014 launched, with the support the Federal and Queensland Governments, a mining and rail project in Queensland's Galilee Basin. The project will have a huge impact in terms of climate change, and on local lands and water. The export of coal through the Great Barrier Reef World Heritage area will greatly diminish the Reef's already precarious capacity to survive.

'River: Contra/indications': Quotes are from 'Drugs in Our Waterways, the Bugs and Beyond' by Bob Wong and Erinn Richmond. https://lens.monash.edu/2018/11/06/1364035/pharmaceuticals-in-our-waterways.

'Space is Blue in Being': Dušan Marek's painting, 'Space', is painted primarily, to my sight, in shades of darker greens that others may see as shades of blue.

'Composed of Light': The painting by Australian artist, Clarice Beckett, referred to in the poem, was painted on the reverse of a Cornflakes box and measures approximately 29.5x32.5cm.

'Is Anyone Anonymous': Indirectly responds to autobiographies by women singers, composers and musicians, particularly Viv

Albertine and Kim Gordon, as well as works by Clara Schumann and Fanny Mendelssohn, and other 19th and 20th century female composers. To state the obvious, women overshadowed by men in their field, or overlooked in their time. It also responds to short videos posted on Twitter, April-May 2020, by Canadian pianist, Angela Hewitt, while she was locked down in London due to Covid 19. One of those pieces was the Aria from Bach's *Goldberg Variations*, being in this case an instrumental piece and not a song. The video only shows Hewitt's hands playing the piano.

Final Note:

'Maria Callas is With Me Tonight': This poem was, unaccountably, left out of my first new and selected volume (my oversight). My sister liked this poem and remarked on its absence at the time. I include it here for various reasons, but specifically to rectify this oversight, and as a small gesture in her memory — Dr Linda Dawson 1954-2022.

www.ingramcontent.com/pod-product-compliance
Lightning Source LLC
Chambersburg PA
CBHW021221090426
42740CB00006B/320